BUILDING CHARACTER ARCS 2 BOOKS IN 1

LEARN AND DEVISE ON THE GO. THE SECRETS TO CREATING CHARACTER ARCS AND CHARACTER ARCS WORKBOOK

JOHN S WARNER

FREE GIFT

Scan the QR code below to claim your gift or visit https://f2edg3.
systeme.io/johnswarner

FOREWORD

All human beings at one stage have tried to use the wrong tool for the job, perhaps you tried as a kid to hit a ball with a stick instead of using a bat, or maybe you've used a knife as a screwdriver to get into a battery compartment on some gadget you own? Or perhaps you did as I did once and tried to use a swivel chair as a ladder to reach a light-bulb and soon discovered it was a bad idea as you lay face down, eating the carpet. Whatever you've tried, I bet my bottom dollar that it would have been easier using the correct tool designed to do the job right.

This book is the right tool, It's the only tool you need to create fantastic characters, but each person can use it differently. You could read it from cover to cover in chronological order learning it all before you try to create anything at all, or if you want, you can skip past the first book and go directly to the workbook and start making characters immediately, and then dip back and forth as you go along. It's entirely your choice. I can't resist creating things, getting straight into the action, and figuring it out as I go. I even try building flatpack furniture without the instructions, although I keep them very close and often use them within 5 minutes. You can do the same with this book; everyone learns through their mistakes, so however you use this book, please get stuck in and enjoy it.

CONTENTS

PART ONE
BOOK 1

Introduction 15
1. THE HOLY TRINITY 19
2. PLOTTING IT OUT 31
3. SCULPTING THE STRUCTURE 45
   a. Freytag's Pyramid: 52
   b. The Hero's Journey: 53
   c. Three-Act Structure: 54
   d. Dan Harmon's Story Circle: 56
   e. Fichtean Curve: 57
   f. Save The Cat! Beat Sheet: 58
   g. Seven-Point Story Structure: 60

4. CHARACTER, NOT CARICATURE 63
5. CREATING YOUR CHARACTER 75
6. YOUR CHARACTER'S JOURNEY 83
7. COMBINING THE LOT 95
8. SUPPORTING CHARACTERS 103
9. DO'S AND DON'TS OF CHARACTER CREATION ... 115
10. TAKING YOUR STORY TO THE NEXT LEVEL ... 125
Conclusion 137

PART TWO
BOOK 2

Introduction 145
1. WHAT'S IN A POSITIVE CHANGE ARC? ... 155
Your Character and Its LIE 156
The character's symptoms of Lie 157
What's the thing your character needs 159
How to know what your character wants 160
Your character meets their ghost 160
Moment of your character's journey 161
The Dilemma of the Normal World 162
Beginning of the First Act 162

Twist of the First Plot Point 162
What happens in the First Half of the Second Act 163
The Turning Point 163
The interesting second half of the second act 164
The Third Plot Point - Ultimate truth? 164
Explore the First half of the Third Act 165
The Most Awaited Climax 165
Building the Resolution 165
Creative Exercises to practice 166

2. THE FLAT ARC 171
The Truth Your Character Believes 172
The Normal World 174
The Characteristic Moment 176
The First Act 187
The First Plot Point 187
The First Half of the Second Act 188
The Midpoint 190
The Second Half Of The Second Act 194
The Third Plot Point 196
The First Half Of The Third Act 197
The Climax 197
The Resolution 200
CREATIVE EXERCISES 204

3. THE NEGATIVE CHANGE ARC TYPE 1:
DISILLUSIONMENT 207
The Lie Your Character Believes 208
The Thing Your Character Needs 210
The Thing Your Character Wants 214
The Characteristic Moment 216
The Normal World 225
The First Act 231
The First Plot Point 235
The First Half of the Second Act 239
The Midpoint 242
The Second Half of the Second Act 244
The Third Plot Point 246
The First Half of the Third Act 246
THE CLIMAX 249
The Resolution 251
Creative Exercises 251

4. THE NEGATIVE CHANGE ARC TYPE 2: FALL — 255

The Lie Your Character Believes — 255

Symptoms of the Lie — 257

Your Character's Ghost — 258

The Thing Your Character Needs — 262

The Thing Your Character Wants — 264

The Characteristic Moment — 267

The Normal World — 271

The First Act — 272

The First Plot Point — 276

The First Half of the Second Act — 278

The Midpoint — 278

The Second Half of the Second Act — 279

The Third Plot Point — 279

The First Half of the Third Act — 279

The Climax — 279

The Resolution — 280

Creative Exercises — 280

5. THE NEGATIVE CHANGE ARC TYPE 3: CORRUPTION — 283

The Truth Your Character Believes — 283

Your Character's Ghost — 285

The Thing Your Character Needs — 285

The Normal World — 285

The Characteristic Moment — 288

The First Act — 294

The First Plot Point — 295

The First Half of the Second Act — 295

The Midpoint — 295

The Second Half of the Second Act — 296

The Third Plot Point — 296

The First Half of the Third Act — 296

The Climax — 297

The Resolution — 297

Creative Exercises — 297

Conclusion — 301

More from John S Warner — 303

Bibliography — 305

PART ONE
BOOK 1

A FICTION WRITER'S GUIDE
TO MASTERFUL CHARACTER CREATION

THE SECRETS TO
CREATING CHARACTER ARCS

(GROWING AUTHORS OUT OF WRITERS)

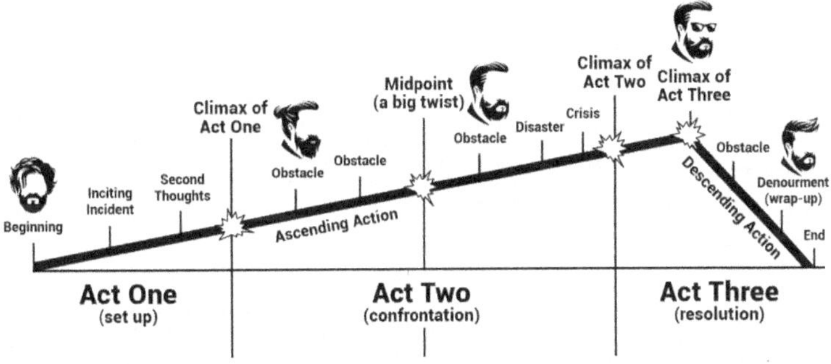

JOHN S. WARNER

INTRODUCTION

"You can never know enough about your characters."

This quote, given by W. Somerset Maugham, explains beautifully the necessity of creating meaningful characters in order for a novel to be successful. And indeed, if you look back to all the books, movies, and shows you have loved in your life, you will find that each had at least one character you could connect with; someone that continued to live on within your heart long after you finished those books, movies, or shows.

Characters are the life of any literary work, be it novels, plays, or short stories. As readers, the first thing that hooks you in a story is when you start caring about its characters.

Once you start caring about the characters, you relate to their thoughts, feelings, and emotions. You will also feel connected to the happenings and events of their lives.

However, as a writer, creating multi-dimensional characters that your readers can relate to is a challenge. Many writers out there would agree that it is, in fact, one of the most difficult parts of writing a story.

Story-writing is a serious job and not something that springs from a mere idea. While the idea is the seed of any story, to turn your story into a full-grown tree, you will need to string all your ideas and thoughts together into a meaningful work.

And even if you manage to power through and complete your story, you will need to have that "wow" factor in order for it to stand out among the countless published stories available to readers. Something that will help your story catch the attention of the audience. This is a stage where many writers feel stuck, which is also a form of writer's block.

If you're a writer with a half-finished book looking for inspiration to move ahead, or someone who wants to write stories but is nervous about where to begin, I understand what you're struggling with.

This book has been written to address the struggles and challenges faced by writers like you. In the chapters ahead, I will discuss the components of a good story. Throughout this journey, I will talk about several strategies and techniques that you can learn that will develop your writing.

The book is designed as a guide for all the writers who have great potential but lack the confidence to write an interesting, engaging story that can keep the readers glued to the pages. It also explains the ideal thought process that can motivate you to write better. Most importantly, it talks about the art of creating character arcs that can keep the readers captivated throughout the story.

If you've already finished writing your story and need guidance for editing it effectively, you will also learn about making final improvements in your story. And in the end, you must be wondering if I'm qualified for the task of writing a book that can serve as your companion during your writing journey. You're right to ask, so let me tell you a little bit about myself.

Born and raised in Oxfordshire in the United Kingdom, I've been studying creative writing and cryptology for over 35 years now. I have two children and am married to a professor who teaches at a local University. Because I've been engaged in creative writing for so many years, both personally and professionally, I have learned a lot about the process and am here to share with you fine people the knowledge and experience I've gathered over the years.

On a personal level, helping other writers with the writing of their novels is a truly satisfying and rewarding experience for me. As an avid reader, I genuinely hope to fill the world with more amazing stories. Not only does it give me great pleasure, but it also strengthens my own confidence in writing. In other words, with your growth and development as a writer, I grow as well.

After spending decades studying creativity, the most priceless lesson I've learned is that no matter how good a writer is, they can always improve and become better at it if they receive the right guidance and advice. And it is my intention to present all writers of the world with an ultimate guide for creating better, more impactful stories.

CHAPTER 1
THE HOLY TRINITY

The concept of the "holy trinity" originated from Christianity, wherein it is believed that the Almighty who protects and blesses its followers is not one single entity: it exists in three different forms. These forms are of the Father, the Son, and the Holy Spirit. And while these three are distinct, they have the same essence or nature.

Just like the three entities that guide believers spiritually in life, a good story is also created with the union of a holy trinity: the union of plot, structure, and characters.

As a writer, you must have asked yourself, "What would make my story a good one?" In this chapter, I aim to answer exactly this question.

The first step to writing any story is to learn about the basic elements of fiction writing. If you have a firm grip on these elements, you will never struggle in planning your story before you start penning it down. But what are these basic elements? They are characters, setting, plot, conflict, point of view, and theme. Once you have clearly defined these elements for your story, the rest of the way will seem significantly easier for you, whether you're writing a novel, a novella, or a short story.

The incorporation of these elements will lend your story the integrity it needs in order to stand out. As a general rule, a good story should answer three main questions:

Whose story is it?

What's happening in the story? What's at stake in the story?

And if you want to make your story great, be sure it answers all of these questions quickly—even in the opening statement itself. Wondering how it's done? Let me show you an example.

The first chapter of Elizabeth George's novel, *What Came Before He Shot Her*, opens with this line:

"Joel Campbell, eleven years old at the time, began his descent towards murder with a bus ride."

This is a great opening for a story because it does two very important things: it introduces the protagonist and sets up the stakes. It tells you whose story it is, what he went through to become a murderer, and why all of it matters.

Readers will want to know more because they have been given information that creates excitement within them. In other words, there's tension in the air about what will happen next if Joel keeps sinking into darkness. And so, readers keep reading!

When you open your story with a hook sentence so full of information about the central plot, your readers will certainly want more.

Another interesting thing about such an opening is that it indicates that the story's plot is moving in the direction of the central action right from the start. It builds your readers' anticipation about learning the answer to the question asked in the title. It's amazing how a single sentence can do so much.

Now, let's return to the concept of the holy trinity we discussed earlier and learn how and why they're important to your story.

PLOT:

A plot is a sequence of events that happens in a story. It's the storyline, which drives the central idea of your story forward. In most cases, there are two types of plots: linear and nonlinear.

In a linear narrative, the main character embarks on a journey or faces an obstacle that they have to overcome before resolving their problem or completing their task. This type of plot is most commonly found in stories involving quests and journeys (for example, *The Lord of The Rings*).

The other form is nonlinear, where multiple characters meet each other on different occasions rather than traveling together on a single road. A nonlinear plot is often seen in detective novels where the investigator must solve a crime. Nonlinear stories can reveal crucial plot points at key moments to maintain the suspense.

Both types of plotting have their own advantages and disadvantages, but most writers use a combination of linear and nonlinear plots to create more engaging stories.

However, it's important to note that no story can be effective without a clear plot. If there is no direction for the story everything becomes chaotic and confusing very quickly. When this happens, readers tend to lose interest before they finish reading your story.

For instance, the Harry Potter series follows a linear structure as Harry faces different obstacles while traveling from one place to another on his quest to defeat Lord Voldemort. It also incorporates elements of nonlinearity by using flashbacks from the past to add more depth and dimension to the narrative.

The main purpose of a plot is to inspire different emotional responses in the readers, making them feel connected to the story. To create an entertaining and wholesome experience for the readers, you must imbue some of these emotions in your plot:

Suspense:

The root of a story's suspense lies in its unpredictability. If your readers don't know what will happen next in the story, it will keep them on the edge of their seats the entire time. There are many ways to create suspense in a story but as an added tip, try to center it around the protagonist because that's who your readers will be most closely connected to.

Anticipation:

Anticipation is another strong emotion that you can use to enhance your plot. But with this emotion, you must tread lightly.

While creating an environment of anticipation in your story can be easily achieved, it is more important to fulfill the anticipation, preferably with a surprising twist. Suppose you keep the readers worried or hopeful for too long without giving them something incredible in the end. In that case, they might feel disappointed and even stop reading it midway.

Surprise:

While a long-drawn-out surprise is a great emotional hook for your readers, sudden twists and turns appeal to them as well. At least once or twice in your story, give your readers something they're not expecting; perhaps a revelation that no one saw coming or a secret that the protagonist is yet to discover.

Empathy:

While surprises and suspense will keep your readers glued to your story, empathy can make it stay with them for the rest of their lives. That is because empathy is one of the most lasting feelings in the world. If your readers can develop feelings of compassion, contempt, or admiration for major or minor characters in the plot, they will always remember your story.

The ultimate job of the plot is to keep the entire story, no matter how long it is, engaging and all events wellconnected; it gives the story a meaning that all readers unconsciously look for. When you develop a striking plot, you ensure that your readers will keep thinking and imagining your story long after they've turned its last page.

STRUCTURE:

In literature, the structure is nothing more than a pattern that keeps your story organized and engaging for the reader.

It provides a framework on which you hang the plot of your story by giving it a unique beginning, middle, and ending.

Before we proceed further, let me clarify one thing: There is no single right way of structuring a story. Every writer has their own writing style and most stories can be structured in more than one way, depending on who is writing it and how they want you to read it.

For example, *The Hobbit* follows the linear structure since it begins in an ordinary place where Bilbo Baggins lives happily, but alone, at Bag End before he is recruited by a party of eager dwarfs and thrust on a journey to recapture their home and defeat the dragon, Smaug. At the end of his adventure, he returns to where he started with many gifts and stories to tell!

On the other hand, novels like *The Catcher in the Rye* follow a nonlinear structure. It begins by describing Holden Caulfield's experiences wandering around New York without any direction or purpose before returning home at the conclusion. Structure builds the foundation for every story, both good and bad, which is why it's important to know how to use it.

For instance, if the structure of your story has an ending that isn't satisfying or surprising enough, it becomes null and void. A poor plot can still be saved by a more robust structure, which is what you must keep in mind while writing your novel!

Structure is the way that presents the events in your book to produce the most enjoyment for your reader, using it to wax and wane the reader's emotions. This variety can make stories gripping to read.

CHARACTERS:

> "If you're inviting people into a story, invite them into all parts of it. Inhabit each character as fully as possible."

This is what Nikole Beckwith, an American playwright and screenwriter, has to say about the characters of a story. But how does one create such wholesome characters? By thinking of them as real people with a full life, and not merely a piece of a fictional work.

The characters that seem most lifelike are often the ones that stay with the readers long after they've finished a book. Now, the real question is: Can you make all the characters of your story lifelike? Many writers would call it nearly impossible, but with practice it's achievable.

E. M. Forster talked about two categories of characters in a story or novel:

flat and **round characters**.

Round characters are central to the plot; without them, there'd be no story. Both the protagonist and antagonist are round characters, while others might include their closest friends or family.

The second category consists of flat characters: the characters that play small or insignificant roles in the story and have no impact on the central plot.

While writing your story, it is the round characters that you need to focus your efforts on. You should describe them and their lives enough to make them well-developed. The better your readers know these characters, the more they'll connect with them.

One thing that all great characters have in common is internal conflict. These characters have a psychological conflict that's often the result of a past experience, either their own or a loved one's. This experience deeply impacts their psyche and is frequently the driving force behind their external conflicts and struggles.

Another essential piece of advice that I will share is to create a list of your character's traits before anything else. It might seem unnecessary since they are created by the writer at will. However, it's important because those details can help you determine the structure and plot that best suits them.

For example, a protagonist with enough flaws will provide readers with many opportunities to become invested in their story while also connecting with them on an emotional level. On the other hand, too many problems can make your main character appear weak or even whiny if not handled properly. Thus, this step is essential for creating characters that "stick" with readers long after they finish reading your story!

A great character is born when the reader starts to relate the character's actions to their past emotional struggles; it is when the reader works out that a character did something a certain way because of what happened in the past. This works best when the reader figures it out by remembering earlier points—not by having things explained to them by the writer. People like to understand others through their own observations.

These three elements—plot, structure, and characters—make up the basic elements of a story. Every writer needs to understand their importance before starting a writing project.

The good news is that they're quite simple to understand, but figuring out how to implement them into your story is where you need to use your creativity.

Understanding the basic elements of fiction books and stories will go a long way toward preparing you to write your own pieces. The key to successful storytelling is understanding the important elements that make a great narrative and incorporating those elements into your writing process at the right time.

Once you figure that out, there's no stopping the flow of fictional stories from your head!

Stories move us only when they allow us to feel how it would be to experience the hero's struggle. Stories have to grab our attention immediately by showing that all is not as it seems and making us feel that we've arrived at a crucial point in the hero's life—when trouble is about to explode.

A great story is designed from beginning to end to answer a single question, and readers expect every word, character, image, and action to move them closer to the answer. The answer, however, should not be obvious. The story will build up to it and make the reader wait until the end for the climax, which is when they discover the answer and feel the full extent of its consequences. You should want to satisfy your readers.

Along with the holy trinity, there are other important elements you need to consider when crafting your story. Let's discuss them in detail:

Point of view:

Knowing your point of view will narrow down who your story is about and focus the narrative.

The protagonist should be defined by what they want, not by what they need, e.g., they want fame but really just need one person to love them. The character's motivation for this goal may shift as the story progresses, but their quest to achieve it must remain true throughout or readers will notice inconsistencies in their actions. It's up to the writer to show why the shift is happening; this is the arc of the character.

The shift can make dramatic sense if, for instance, the hero falls in love with someone along the way because that love provides them with a new emotional door into life. However, it can't happen miraculously out of nowhere! The shift has to be logical within the context of your story. Therefore, you'll need to plan ahead and figure out where and how you want your character's journey to change. Most stories show the protagonist chasing what they want and ending up with what they need as a natural progression; it works time and again.

But I digress. The point of view of your story decides from whose perspective the novel is written. Whoever this person is, your readers will see the story through their eyes. There are three points of view that you can use in your story.

- First-person perspective is where the narrator refers to themselves using the term "I." Although this perspective was initially used mainly in autobiographies, nowadays, many fiction writers tend to use it as well. This perspective helps the readers empathize with the narrator. The protagonist and the reader discover things at the same time. Although the reader may try to think ahead and work out the plot—people can't help themselves and it can make it fun.
- Second-person perspective is where the narrator narrates the story in a conversational manner, using "you." This perspective is commonly seen in nonfiction or self-help books and is best avoided in fiction stories as it can lead to confusion unless you have a particular purpose in mind. It's a descriptive way of writing that leans toward self-help books but could be used creatively, depending on your story.
- Third-person perspective is where the narrator speaks from the perspective of a third person, often the protagonist, referring to them as "he," "she," or "they." This narrative style has the advantage of flexibility over the other perspectives and is, therefore, seen often in fiction stories. It enables you to be anyone or everyone in the story.

Setting:

The setting of your story is important for two major reasons. First, you need to be aware of the period and any major historical events surrounding it because they may influence your characters' actions.

Secondly, you need to understand where your story takes place in order to describe its landmarks and use sensory details that truly evoke how it looks, feels, or even smells.

You don't have to have a setting that is precise with a name. It can just be a cabin in the middle of the woods. Just know in your head where it is so you can describe it. The key is to describe something in a way that triggers the reader emotionally without effort. Usually, the least amount of words to get to this emotional feeling is the best approach.

Thomas Harris, who wrote *The Silence of the Lambs*, is a master at this:

"But the face on the pillow, rosy in the firelight, is certainly that of Clarice Starling, and she sleeps deeply, sweetly, in the silence of the lambs."

Create a word picture with vivid, sensory detail that allows readers to feel the setting. Different types of fiction often take place in a variety of settings. For example:

- Realistic fiction: Set in our world, where story elements are treated as if they were real so readers can easily relate to them.
- Fantasy: A secondary world where magic could exist but also has rules governing this magical realm (like not being able to go back in time to change the past, etc.).
- Science fiction: A secondary world where either science or technology has advanced beyond our current level, making events in this world seem fantastical to readers.
- Historical fiction: All story elements are set in the past and based on real people. It will be based on historical events but dialogue will be invented by the writer, giving your protagonist an older point of view than what people have now.
- Contemporary fiction: Much like realistic fiction but it also takes place in recent times (from the 60s onward).

Narrative:

The narrative includes the descriptions surrounding the dialogue. It tells readers what is happening when there are no characters around to act out the scene. And it is important because, like with every story element, you can use it as a tool to manipulate your readers' emotions.

Mesh these two elements together by using sensory details (touch, smell) to make an experience more vivid and powerful. Your narrative describes the people, the scene, the emotions, and actions without revealing everything. It tries to put the reader there, enveloped within the story.

Style:

Style is the way your story is written. It involves how the sentences are put together, the type of words used, and the emotional and descriptive impact the writing brings.

Even a simple story can be told in a stylistic way if the right words are chosen. And you should always take care to ensure that your writing is clear and understandable. Don't use flowery language or try too hard to make it sound "deep" or clever by straining for effect. George Orwell's *Animal Farm* was written simply with basic vocabulary and yet it stands as a classic all these years later.

Theme:

The theme is what your story is about. It's a statement of belief about life and how it works. It gives readers a reason for why they should care about this story, which means it has to be something they want to think about.

Don't bore your reader by explaining the theme as it unfolds through the story or tell readers what you're trying to say with the story.

Instead, weave the themes into the text as part of your storytelling so that readers can discover them on their own. If one of your themes is love, for example, then your readers should feel this while reading for themselves, you shouldn't have to force an explanation on people, the theme should reveal itself.

Now that we've covered the basic groundwork of the elements that make a good story, let's explore each element of the holy trinity in-depth, starting with the plot.

CHAPTER 2
PLOTTING IT OUT

"A life without purpose is like a novel without a plot. It wanders all over the place, is hard to follow, and in the end, doesn't get particularly good reviews."

In these two sentences, Dr. Mardy Grothe, an American psychologist, has summed up the entire meaning of the plot beautifully. In any work of fiction, be it a short story or a long novel, the plot is always the backbone, supporting different events that come together and presenting the readers with a story they will never forget.

If you're new to the world of writing, the first thing you must learn is that there is no story without a plot. If you're writing a story without first constructing a plot to follow while composing it, your story might not achieve the desired effect on its readers.

And what, really, is the purpose of a story? To provide the readers with an emotional experience that will resonate within them. In crafting a plot what you are really doing is arranging a story's events in an order that will evoke intense emotions (interest, suspense, anticipation, curiosity, surprise, thrill, and empathy) in your readers so that they are lifted out of their own lives into your captivating story. The more thought you put into the plot, the more lasting the effect the story will have on your readers. Now, before we delve deeper into the importance of the plot, let's quickly discuss what it is.

The most common definition of a plot is "a series of events that form a story." This story could either be in the form of a novel, a movie, or a TV series. Regardless of what form a story is being presented in, it must have a plot.

Now, there are many series of events that tell a story in our daily lives. Perhaps you might have seen a cute kitten being rescued from the roof of a building on your way to work, or your son may have learned something new and interesting at school today. These kinds of things are happening around us all the time. But do all of them have the potential to make a good story? Not necessarily.

These basic daily happenings are often common to many people, including your potential readers. Therefore, they are unlikely to find themselves drawn to it. If these people wanted to read about the mundane happenings of daily life, what would they gain from it?

Let me give you a little insight into the minds of your readers. They read fiction because, more often than not, they lead simple lives with occasional or no adventures. To them, stories are a means to escape the mundanity of their lives and lose themselves in thrilling stories.

Another reason behind reading fiction is to evoke an emotional response to tragic or fantastical happenings in the story. If you fail to provide them with any of these elements through your story, you cannot be a successful writer.

Therefore, when you're about to structure the plot of your story, you must ensure that it has a captivating, unusual hook that can appeal to the readers; give them something new and strange to think about.

For instance, take the *Hunger Games* series. The story contains no new elements like aliens or superhuman creatures. The author has based it on humans and yet created a plot so extraordinary that the entire world felt drawn to it. The concept of a cruel, dictating Capitol that rules the twelve districts cruelly and forces their citizens to participate in a dangerous game of death solely to assert their authority is not something you find every day. And, thus, the books gained immense popularity as soon as they were published. While designing the plot of your story, make sure to give it something unusual that can evoke the deepest emotions in your readers.

Suppose you've sat down with your laptop or notebook to create a plotline; do you feel clueless about where to start? Don't worry—you're not alone. In order to give you a direction and get you moving, I'll now talk about some pointers that can help in the construction of your plot.

- **Your plot should provide a smooth flow to the story.** As we've discussed earlier, a plot is a series of events that, when combined, makes the whole story. The key to a great story lies in a smooth plot. Your plot should have a sense of continuity in it, wherein one event is connected to the next one in a manner that they all make absolute sense when brought together. The task becomes more difficult in a longer story, which is why you should structure your plot accordingly. This doesn't mean to say the story has to be linear from start to finish, just that each plot point should move the story forward.
- **The focus of your plot should be on the leading characters of your story.** You must remember that your leading characters are central to the story and, therefore, the plot. There might be as many as one hundred characters in your story or as few as ten. However, you cannot delve deeply into each character. It is always best to give your readers a better insight into your protagonist's character rather than familiarizing them with each character a little bit. Furthermore, even when you're describing the protagonist, focus your attention on the events and experiences that are directly relevant to the plot to provide a single direction to the story. Drip feed your main character's motivation which in turn forms the plot.
- **Your plot should have a clear insight into your protagonist's psyche.** Like all good stories, your story must also have a climax point; it could be a monumental, life-altering decision

or an unfortunate event. Whatever it is, when the actions of the protagonist are involved, you should give your readers a look into their psyche; show them how they came to that decision, what motivated them. It will make the readers feel like they know the protagonist personally, therefore, creating a bond. Try and convey your main character's motivation by describing their actions rather than describing their feelings: show don't tell.

- **The plot of your story should start with a bang.** Your readers like nothing better than an abrupt start to a story that will shake their worlds (not literally, of course.) A story that starts slow might lose the interest of the readers well before the arrival of a twist. However, a story that starts with a bang (or a fantastic situation) holds a lot of promise for the readers, keeping them captivating until the very end. If you keep this in mind while constructing your plot, your story will certainly be a hit among your readers. A mystery works as well as a bang; an unanswered, puzzling situation can hook the reader just as well. The start of a story is the most likely point where people will lose interest; readers aren't emotionally connected with your characters at the start and can just stop reading if they don't feel entertained.

- **Your plot should grab the emotions of your readers, but let go in the end.** As a reader, when you read a story, a part of your brain plays it like it's your own experience; it is how you connect with stories. As a writer, to give your readers a connecting hook, you must give them a plot that stirs their strongest emotions, such as ecstasy, sorrow, or anxiety. And while thrills are a part of every good story, you should never end yours with one. If there's something readers hate the most, it's the stories that have no sense of completion in the end. Creating a cliff-hanger for a sequel is one thing, but you must give them something they can hold on to and acknowledge the end properly. Otherwise, they will never think of your story with fond memories or recommend it to their friends. It's a tried-and-tested formula. In short, most people don't like loose ends, so try to wrap them up in a satisfying way.

If you follow these pointers, you will certainly be successful in creating a brilliant plotline for your story.

However, your job doesn't end as soon as you're done with building the plot. Once your plot is ready, you should also examine it to see whether it's an ideal outline for your story or not. Every good plot must have three essential qualities, for which you can check yours during the examining process.

The Nucleus: First and foremost, no matter how diverse the plot is, it should have a single defining point: the nucleus. One event, one question, one decision on which the entire action of the story is based. And to make your story even better, you should put this defining moment earlier in the story and then show its consequences moving forward.

For instance, in Jennifer Niven's book *All the Bright Places*, the action of the story starts with Violet trying to kill herself by jumping from the ledge of a bell tower. Later in the novel, it is learned that she was depressed because of her sister's death, and then we see her dealing with it eventually.

Good Reason: The second requirement of a good plot is reason or logic. While it is true that fictional works needn't stick to the laws of the real world, even they must follow basic reason or logic. Many writers, particularly beginners, make the mistake of writing a nonsensical story while trying to create something different or extraordinary. Although differences are generally appreciated in the world of fiction, if it has no link to anything your readers can relate to, it defeats its own purpose. For example, imagine your character's childhood dog is killed by the antagonist and your main character just shrugs it off; people would find it hard to relate to that character after that. A well-developed character is believable.

The Drama: You might have often heard that a good story always keeps the readers on the edge of their seats. It is the last rule you should follow while examining your plot. Ask yourself these questions: Does my plot have enough unexpected twists, drama, or conflicts to keep the readers interested? Or is it too plain? If the latter is the case with your plot, it's time to make some changes.

DIFFERENT TYPES OF PLOTS:

Now, let's move to talk about categorizing your plot. The nature of your plot describes which category it would fall in. According to Christopher Booker, a well-known author and journalist, there are seven different types of plots that ultimately decide the genre of the story.

Tragedy:

In a tragedy, your protagonist is fundamentally good but has a major or minor character flaw that ultimately leads to their downfall. Such plots often begin on a happy note but end rather sadly.

Some popular tragedies are *Romeo and Juliet, Oedipus Rex,* and *The Great Gatsby.*

Comedy:

Comic plots have a light and humorous essence throughout. The climax of these plots is often any adverse circumstance that is ultimately resolved by the protagonist. *Four Weddings and a Funeral* and *A Midsummer Night's Dream* are examples of comedy in fiction.

The Quest:

These fictional pieces are centered around a journey to obtain an important object or reach a destination, which is the hero's ultimate goal. Throughout their journey, they might face several temptations or challenges that they need to overcome.

The Lord of the Rings is one of the best examples of quest fiction.

Voyage and Return:

This type of plot is quite similar to the last one, with one major difference. In quests, it is not necessary to find the protagonist returning to their point of origin, while in voyage and return, the "return" is almost as essential as the journey itself.

The moral of these literary works lies in the lessons learned by the protagonist on the journey. *Gone with the Wind*, *Alice's Adventures in Wonderland*, and *Gulliver's Travels* are all based on the voyage and return plot.

Overcoming the Monster:

These plots always deal with a long-drawn-out battle between a protagonist and an antagonist, who is probably threatening their family or homeland. In the end, the protagonist always emerges victorious.

Some fine examples of these plots include *Star Wars*, *Dracula*, and all of the James Bond novels.

Rags to Riches:

One of the most common plotlines, wherein the protagonist is initially poor and miserable but comes across wealth and prosperity by chance, only to lose it all again in the climax. In the later part, they work hard and regain all that they'd lost, becoming a wiser person in the process and realizing that it's not riches that make you happy, it's the things that money can't buy.

Popular bedtime stories like *Cinderella* and *The Prince and the Pauper* are based on these plots.

Rebirth:

These plots don't deal with a literal rebirth but a metaphorical one, where the protagonist is initially bitter and unkind, either naturally or forced by their brutal fate. However, a life-altering event changes them and helps them become a better person in the end.

Popular examples using these plots are *Beauty and the Beast*, *Pride and Prejudice*, and *The Frog Prince*.

While building a plot might seem quite simple in theory, in truth, it's a much more complicated job. However, once done with precision, it will ensure that your story will become a potential best-seller.

If you're struggling with creating a plot that seems just right to you, here are five golden rules that I follow:

- **Start by drawing a plot skeleton.** Your skeleton would essentially need only two parts: a complication and its resolution. In the story, there might be something that your protagonist is looking for but can't find; this is your complication. In the end, they must get it somehow, which is the resolution. The "how" and "why" in between constitute the whole plot. Once you've figured out the complication and resolution, the skeleton of your plot is ready. **Fleshing out the plot comes next.** While creating the skeleton, you've already found and answered the main question asked in your story. But good stories need more than just a climax to make sense. There must be other, smaller, but vital instances, changes, and events that add more value to the story. These provide flesh to your plot skeleton, taking your story one step ahead. Your protagonist is taking each step along their arc to reach the final goal.
- **A strong plot resolution is vital.** A plot resolution is basically everything that happens in your story after the point of climax. After building up your story to this point, you can't let it fall to a flat end; your readers will hate that. Therefore, giving the plot a strong and sensible direction after the climax point is paramount.
- **Let the story end naturally.** As readers near the end of the story, they wouldn't want it to be dragged out unnecessarily. Therefore, past the point of resolution, you must try to wrap up your story as quickly as you can. I must confess that although I enjoyed the movies considerably, the ending to *The Lord of the Rings* trilogy, in my opinion, dragged on for thirty minutes longer than it should. If you felt the same you understand what I mean. Once you are wrapped up it's time to go.

- **Are your protagonists independent?** While all readers enjoy a good twist, introducing a new character or creating an unprecedented random event simply to help your protagonist look more exciting is a bad idea if it's too late in the story. If your readers connect with your protagonist, they'd like to see them tackle their problems by themselves. Basically don't add a new main character too near to the end. Readers find it discombobulating and, for that reason, it is rarely done.

PLOT POINT:

If you're new to the world of writing, you may not have heard about plot points before. Remember how we learned that a plot is a series of events that together form a story? Well, plot points are every single event or incident in your story that propels it in a single direction. These points have the responsibility of moving your characters forward in the story and helping them grow.

Are you wondering how plot points are different from the plot? It's quite simple; while any event in your story can be part of the plot, only the events that are significant to its movement or flow can be regarded as a plot point. You can think of them as the nuts and bolts that hold your story together, keeping it from falling apart. They are the key points.

Any good story should contain seven plot points (from beginning to end) that mark the highs and lows of your narrative. These are:

- Inciting Incident:

Also called a "hook," the inciting incident is the first significant point of change in the protagonist's life, which will also give the readers an idea of what the main conflict of the story is going to be. This point should ideally be placed in the second chapter of your story so that the readers can get to know and sympathize with your protagonist before they learn about it. Let's use *Back to the Future* as an example of these plot points. The hook would be when the protagonist Marty McFly is sent back to 1955 in a time machine made from a DeLorean car.

- First Plot Point:

The first plot point comes as a consequence of the initial hook. It is often a conflict that pushes the protagonist to take action, either a good or a bad one. It is also referred to as "the point of no return." In *Back to the Future* the first plot point is when Marty discovers from Doc Brown that he literally can't return home because there is nothing to power the time machine and that he has accidentally altered time by preventing his future parents from meeting.

- First Pinch Point:

The first pinch point comes right in the middle of the story. It is a significant moment in which the protagonist makes a critical decision. In *Back to the Future*, Marty must devise a plan to get his future mother and father to fall in love.

- Midpoint:

Although midpoint comes after half of the story is already over, it has been so named because it brings the realization that the struggles dealt with so far were inconsequential. The midpoint brings with it a contextual shift, giving room to far greater troubles. It also pushes the protagonists, renewing their zeal to fight and overcome these troubles. In *Back to the Future* Marty and Doc realize they have to use a bolt of lightning at exactly the right time to get Marty back to the future and repair the changes to the timeline involving his future parents before he can go back.

- Final Pinch Point:

The final pinch point brings forward another pressure point from the initial conflict, often with a small failure on the protagonist's part. This pinch point often gives a different direction to the entire story, creating an unexpected twist. In *Back to the Future* the complications while trying to get his parents together create a situation where his future father George knocks out the school bully with an unexpected left hook.

- Second Plot Point:

Also referred to as the "final plot point," the second plot point marks the lowest phase of your protagonist's life, where it seems like they've lost all hope and are defeated. This point might give your readers a sense that this is how the story ends. In *Back to the Future*, with just seconds to go before the lightning strikes, the wires from the clock tower become disconnected, meaning that Marty's chance of return is surely lost.

- Resolution:

As the name itself indicates, the resolution is basically the point of completion where the main conflict is resolved, and the protagonist achieves peace and happiness. In other words, the resolution brings a satisfying conclusion to your story. In *Back to the Future* Marty returns home and his parents are in love and everything is back to normal with the added bonus that his father seems more confident due to his defeat of the bully, Biff, and his life seems better.

Now that you've developed a basic understanding of plot points, you can easily incorporate them into your plot to strengthen it further and make your story richer and more compelling. If you're still confused about how to add plot points to your story, check out these pointers:

- **Choose plot points that provide an emotional foundation to your story.** You should draw these points from the wishes and desires of your protagonists, as your readers will connect with them the most and want to learn more about their thought processes.
- **Ensure that each plot point is a point of no return.** The job of plot points is to push the story forward and not backward. Therefore, you must assign these points to incidents that are irreversible to the protagonists.

- **Build plot points around structural intervals.** Pick a place (the end of a chapter or its beginning) to place these points. It will provide a patterned movement to the plot and keep your readers more engaged, eagerly waiting for the next one.
- **Create an outline in the beginning.** Before elaborating on your plot points, draw a rough outline of where they will be placed. This will provide you with a roadmap you can follow while writing the story.

A wise man once said that you can never add too much excitement to your plot. If you're of the same mindset, here are more ways that can elevate your plot in ways you couldn't have imagined:

- Use subplots to provide more depth to your plot. The subplots can give your readers more insight into the different characters of your story and highlight the themes you're presenting.
- Create more conflicts or tension to keep the readers guessing whether or not the protagonist will make it through. Physical dangers aren't necessary but can certainly give you an edge. The early addition of new characters that are secondary to the plot can also help you achieve this.
- Add complications to the history of past experiences of your leading characters (either protagonists or antagonists).
- Add more personality to non-living things, such as a house, a college, or a workplace.
- Keep reminding your readers at regular intervals about what's at stake.
- Make your protagonists feel like they're running out of time. It can elevate the thrill among the readers as nothing else can. A countdown to a major event drives your story forward and forces you to wrap up loose ends.

As we near the end of the chapter, let me remind you that writing is about more than simply reading how to write. With that being said, here's a simple task you can practice that will help you create a story using a plot outline. I'm going to assign four tasks to you:

- Write down ten events or happenings that have the potential to spark a story, no matter how small. This could be something that happened to you, a friend, a family member, or even something you read in a magazine or watched on TV.
- Create ten fictional characters drawn from your life or experiences. You can manifest them from your workspace, home, or friend circle. In fact, you can draw from someone you've read about in your textbooks or heard about from your teachers, parents, or grandparents. If you're more creative, you might even create characters out of thin air.
- Write the basic outline of ten stories. These stories could be ones that you've heard from your ancestors, old folktales, or even the myths in your culture. You needn't write the whole story; just sum it up in a couple of sentences.
- Once you've prepared these lists, pick one item from each list, and use them to write a short story. This will get your creative juices flowing.

Go ahead and see how it turns out. Good luck!

CHAPTER 3
SCULPTING THE STRUCTURE

How would you define the term "structure"? Its standard definition states that it is the arrangement of and relations between parts or elements of something complex.

Now, when you relate this definition to story writing, you'd find that your story is "something complex," and the arrangement of your story is its structure. In other words, the structure is the skeletal framework upon which a story is built. The purpose of designing the structure of a story is to derive the maximum impact from its plot. It helps a writer present their story in a clear, palatable, and exciting progression to keep the readers engaged until the very end.

As you can imagine, designing the structure for a short story is much simpler than designing it for a longer story. The structure in short stories has less room for variability than in longer stories like novels or novellas.

There are several ways in which you structure your story:

- A story that begins in the present and will remain in the present throughout the course of it. A story that's based over weeks and not years.
- A story that begins in the present but will move between

present and past to give your readers a clear insight into the story's meaning.

- A story that follows a linear chronological progression. Characters grow old along the way. A story that moves consistently in both time and space to provide the readers a better understanding of all characters.

Many of you might have noticed how similar the structure seems to the plot so far. And I agree, these elements can often seem confusing to any writer in the beginning. Therefore, in the next section, I will attempt to explain their differences.

THE DIFFERENCE BETWEEN PLOT AND STRUCTURE:

While both plot and structure play an indispensable role in story writing, they are significantly different from one another. The plot—the series of events that form a story—is simply a description of what will happen in your story. On the other hand, the structure defines how you will narrate or present the story to the readers.

A General Rule:

As a general rule, the plot of a story is always constructed in a linear manner, while the structure needn't adhere to any such constraint. It can be linear or jump between time and places, as I've already mentioned earlier. This is exactly why the plot always comes before structure. Once you've laid out all events of your story sequentially (plot), you can choose how to tell it to the readers for maximum impact by structuring it accordingly.

The plot of the story is restrictive, while its structure can be more abstract. Your structure decides how the story is broken into each chapter and divided into sections, when and how the conflict and climax are to be presented, and how you present the resolution in the end. Let me give you an example of how plot and structure are different. I'm sorry if this is a spoiler but the movie *The Sixth Sense* is over twenty years old so I'm going to risk it. If you had discovered that Bruce Willis's character Malcolm Crowe had died at the start of the plot then the story wouldn't have worked at all. The whole movie works because you don't know he is a ghost. It's structured to maximize enjoyment.

Another essential difference between plot and structure is that while almost all works of fiction have a unique plot, you needn't come up with something new every time to provide them with a structure. All you need to do is to obtain a thorough understanding of the common story structures and devices that will help you develop better stories. I hope any confusion you had regarding the plot and structure has been clarified now. Think of the plot as a train line that runs from A to B and think of the structure as a rollercoaster that's built from all the sections of the track placed in the best order to create the most enjoyment.

THE NECESSITY OF STRUCTURE:

As a young writer, I often wondered why the structure was considered essential for a story. If I could create a story from its plot alone, what was the need to go through the trouble of designing a structure?

Why Bother?

I'm sure many of you must be asking that same question right about now. To answer your question, let me tell you something that I've learned from my experience in creative writing. No matter how interesting or well-written your plot might be, it is very likely to turn out boring when you start constructing your story on it. Wondering why? It is because, while a story might seem exciting when it is summed up in 500 to 1,000 words, when you extend the same to 30,000 or 60,000 words it will become impossible to retain the interest of your readers.

Ask yourself this: As a reader, would you want to read a plain, linear story that stretches so long? Perhaps not. To keep you engaged in a story that long, the plot itself is not sufficient.

Here's where structure comes in. It is the job of structure to add appeal to your story. While the plot defines the events that will take place in your story, the structure will decide how these events came to be; it shows the decisions and choices of the characters that lead to any event. And in the end, these choices will give your readers insight into your characters' psyches and help form a bond or connection with them.

For instance, take the Harry Potter series. J. K. Rowling has done an exceptional job of creating a plotline unlike any other for the series. But do you think the books would've gained as much popularity if she hadn't used the structural devices that she did? Unlikely. Without its structure, the whole series would be one long-drawn-out story leading Harry to the ultimate war with Lord Voldemort in the final book.

STRUCTURING YOUR STORY:

When you sit down to design the structure of your story for the first time, you might feel blank in the beginning, with no clue about how to cut and assemble the story to impact your readers most profoundly.

A decent place to start is by asking yourself these four basic questions about the story:

- **What is the character arc of your protagonist?** Your protagonist is the center of the whole story and, naturally, the character your readers want to know most closely. This is why their character arc is the first thing you should start working on. Think about what you want them to be like, the changes they will undergo throughout the story, the events that will lead to these changes, and the character development from them. We'll discuss character arcs more extensively in Chapter 6.
- **Is the narrator of your story in the first or third person?** The first- and third-person perspectives are most commonly used when writing a long story. And while first person can be quite restrictive, third person offers you more flexibility to move your narrative in nonlinear, circular, or parallel styles. Therefore, my advice to first-time authors would be to stick to the third-person narrative. However, if you feel like the first-person perspective is more appropriate for your story, you can always use monologues and flashbacks or diary entries to add more appeal to the linear structure of your story.

- **What would be the major events in your story?** Every story should have seven major touchpoints: starting point, inciting incident, rising action, turning point, climax, falling point, and the final resolution. Identifying what events will be placed in these touchpoints should be the next step of structuring your story. Once you've identified these touchpoints, you can decide whether these can be presented in a non-traditional structure which can give your story an edge over other stories.

- **How many perspectives are you planning to feature in the story?** In my personal opinion, adding multiple perspectives to a story lends a diversity that any reader would be attracted to. This technique not only gives them more insight into different characters but also allows them more space to form their opinions. Virginia Woolf's novel, *To the Lighthouse*, is a perfect example of a multiperspective work of fiction.

Once you've answered all these questions, you will be able to pick a structure template that's most well-suited to your story. There are five structure templates that a number of screenwriters and novelists have developed over time. Let's take a look at these templates before moving ahead.

1. **Linear Structure:**

Also referred to as the chronological structure, the linear structure is the most commonly used structure template in all fictional works, including books, plays, movies, and TV shows. In this structure, the story is presented in chronological order. However, the characters can still remember their past in flashbacks in these works.

The Harry Potter series is a perfect example of novels written in a linear structure.

1. **Nonlinear / Fractured Structure:**

The nonlinear structure is also known as a fractured structure, as these narratives often jump outside of chronological order. These stories can often begin with the end, and then the rest of the story unfolds.

Alice McDermott's *Charming Billy* and David Mitchell's *Cloud Atlas* are some of the finest works with this structure template.

1. **Circular Structure:**

In a circular structure, a story begins and ends at the same point, as all events and imagery ultimately reach the story's starting point.

Long Night Moon by Cynthia Rylant is a novel written in a circular structure.

1. **Parallel Structure:**

When multiple storylines unfold and run simultaneously in a story, it's based on a parallel structure. All these storylines are generally tied together by a theme, character, or event.

F. Scott Fitzgerald's *The Great Gatsby* also follows this structure.

5. Interactive Structure:

Although not used in classic literature, it is, nevertheless, a form of structure. In an interactive structure template, the readers can access various interactive storylines that they can select in a book. Children's books are often structured on this template, such as the *Choose Your Own Adventure* series.

Now that you've answered the key questions of your story's structure and chosen the right template for it, you're already halfway to completion. Here are some more tips that can lead you the rest of the way:

- **Organize the narrative into a three-act structure.** All stories have three parts—beginning, middle, and end—which is exactly what the three-act structure is all about. Breaking your story into these three acts will smooth the flow of your structure. The first act would open with an inciting incident, giving way to rising action, leading to the second act's climax. This climax will de-escalate in the falling action of the third act, which ends in the final resolution. **Create an outline of what your readers should know about the characters and when.** The backstories and personalities of your leading characters are what fascinate your readers the most. Now, you can serve it all to them at once, or you can stretch it out, handing them little pieces of insight every now and then to keep them wanting more. A proper outline made beforehand will help you execute it more efficiently while writing the story. Backstories that are drip-fed to the reader seem more natural than all at once.

- **Be careful of loose ends.** Nothing can spoil a good story more than loose ends. And as you might already know, the possibility of loose ends grows tremendously when you write a longer story. To make sure that it doesn't happen with your story, you must keep track of all the potential questions you're raising for your readers and answer them at the right time in the story

.

DIFFERENT TYPES OF STORY STRUCTURES:

While we've already discussed different structure templates above, what I will talk about now are the seven types of story structures that you must know about as a writer. Furthermore, I will also elaborate on the major components of these structures that can help you incorporate these in your story. Once you've worked out your plot you can find the structure that works best with your plot points. Don't worry if it starts to look complicated, almost like a restaurant menu with too much choice on it, as I've said your plot will dictate the structure. Let's get to it:

A. FREYTAG'S PYRAMID:

Freytag's pyramid was named after Gustav Freytag, a famous German novelist and playwright. This pyramid-like structure is based on the classic Greek tragedies of Euripides and Sophocles but it isn't very popular in the modern storytelling culture. This is because the model ends in catastrophe, something readers don't seek in books or movies anymore.

Arthur Miller's *Death of a Salesman* is a play that follows Freytag's pyramid structure.

Freytag's pyramid has these five dramatic points:

Introduction—where the inciting incident takes place after the status quo has been established. Rising action—the stakes heighten as the protagonist actively chases their goal.

Climax—becomes a point of no return to the status quo for the protagonist.

Fall—presents the aftermath of the climax; as the story moves forward from this point, the tension runs high.

Catastrophe—brings the protagonist to their lowest point, where all their worst fears come true.

B. THE HERO'S JOURNEY:

The structure of the hero's journey is provided by Christopher Vogler, who was inspired by Joseph Campbell's concept of monomyth before designing it. As its name suggests, the structure follows an adventurous journey of a protagonist, often on a quest for an object or destination.

George Lucas's *Stars Wars* is based on this plot structure.

Vogler has divided this structure into the following twelve steps:

- The Ordinary World—gives an insight into the present, normal life of the hero.
- The Call of Adventure—presents the inciting incident; an opportunity for the hero to set out on an extraordinary journey.
- Refusal of the Call—shows how the hero is reluctant to take on such an adventure.

- Meeting the Mentor—hero meets an authoritative figure (a hermit, wizard, or teacher) who guides and prepares them for what they are about to face. Crossing the First Threshold—signifies the hero's first step into a new world.
- Tests, Allies, Enemies—the hero is surrounded by challenges, amidst which they meet new friends. Approach to the Inmost Cave—the hero achieves something remarkable, marking their first victory of sorts.
- The Ordeal—they come face-to-face with the biggest challenge of their life.
- Reward—marks the attainment of a remarkable prize (often a tool or weapon, like a sword) that brings the hero one step closer to final victory. The Road Back—the hero realizes that the reward was perhaps a wrong choice; more challenges lie in wait.
- Resurrection—brings forth a climactic test of everything that has been learned so far; the hero meets the true challenge.
- Return with the Elixir—marks the hero's final victory, after which they return to their regular old life.

C. THREE-ACT STRUCTURE:

The three-act structure is based on the basic idea that we discussed earlier. It divides the entire story into three parts: beginning, middle, and end.

L. Frank Baum's *The Wonderful Wizard of Oz* is based on the three-act structure.

THREE-ACT STRUCTURE

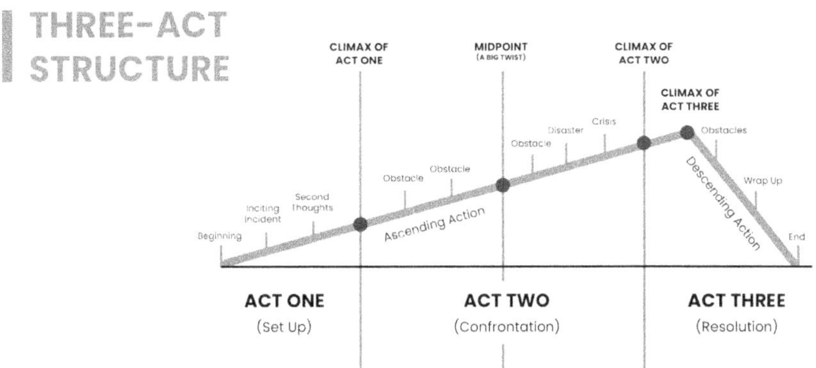

Act 1: Set-up

This act is further divided into three parts: the exposition, where we are introduced to the world of the story; the inciting incident; and the first plot point, where the protagonist crosses the threshold setting the plot into motion.

Act 2: Confrontation

The first part of this act comprises the rising action, where we are familiarized with the new world of the protagonist, who also finds new friends and enemies at this point.

Then comes the midpoint, which adds a twist to the protagonist's mission.

The last part of the act brings the second plot point, wherein the protagonist fails, which makes the reader question their ability to succeed in the end.

Act 3: Resolution

The third act begins with a pre-climax, which is the darkest time for the protagonist. It is at this point that they must be strong and choose to act.

The pre-climax is followed by the climax, where the protagonist is faced with the antagonist one last time. There's a wild tension about who will In the last part of the act, or the denouement, we know how the climax ended and are introduced to a new status quo. All loose ends are also tied up here before the story comes to a close.

D. DAN HARMON'S STORY CIRCLE:

Dan Harmon, the co-creator of the TV series *Rick and Morty*, has created a new story structure, also drawing inspiration from Campbell's monomyth structure. This structure has been used in several episodes of *Rick and Morty*.

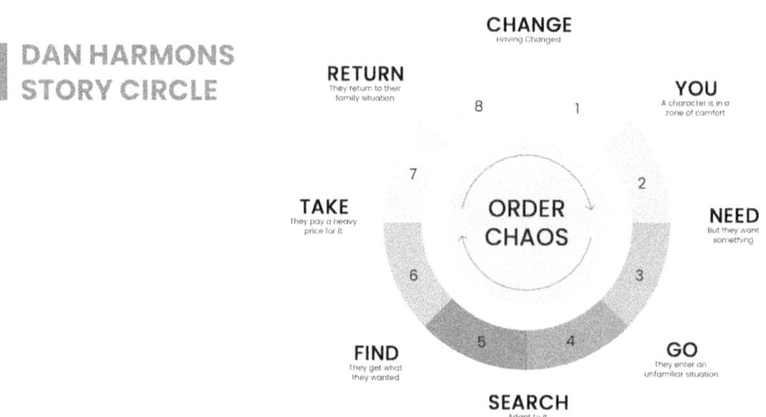

This circle is divided into eight parts:

- A character is in their comfort zone—the status quo is established here.
- But they want something—the inciting incident is introduced here.
- They enter an unfamiliar situation—the character
- realizes that they must do something new in order to achieve what they want.

- They adapt to it—they face several struggles and challenges and eventually begin to succeed. And get what they want—this is generally a false victory.
- They pay a hefty price for it—here, the protagonist realizes that what they wanted wasn't what they truly needed.
- And return to their comfort zone—having learned this truth, they decide that it's time to head back. Having changed—this change could either be for better or worse.

E. FICHTEAN CURVE:

The Fichtean curve is a narrative structure derived from John Gardner's *The Art of Fiction*. It contains a series of obstacles in the protagonist's path, leading to the ultimate climax.

Everything I Never Told You, the work of Celeste Ng, is a perfect example of the Fichtean Curve. There are three parts to this structure:

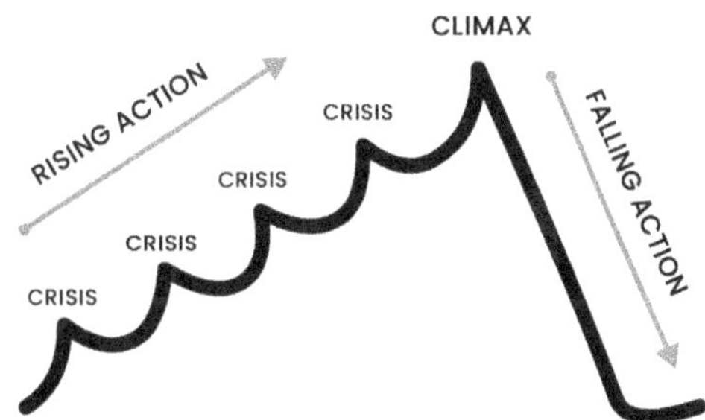

- Rising action

The rising action is divided into five parts here. The first part, the inciting incident, opens the story with a tragedy or a crisis, which is then heightened or gets worse gradually over the next four parts.

- Climax

The climax comes toward the end of the story, where the reason or truth behind the first tragedy is revealed to the readers.

- Falling action

As the readers confront the climax, they achieve some level of resolution and get a look at the new life of the story's characters as the story comes to an end.

F. SAVE THE CAT! BEAT SHEET:

The *Save the Cat!* beat sheet template was created by the famous screenwriter Blake Snyder. And although Snyder had inspiration for this narrative from the three-act structure, he added his own unique touch. This structure is quite popular across different media platforms.

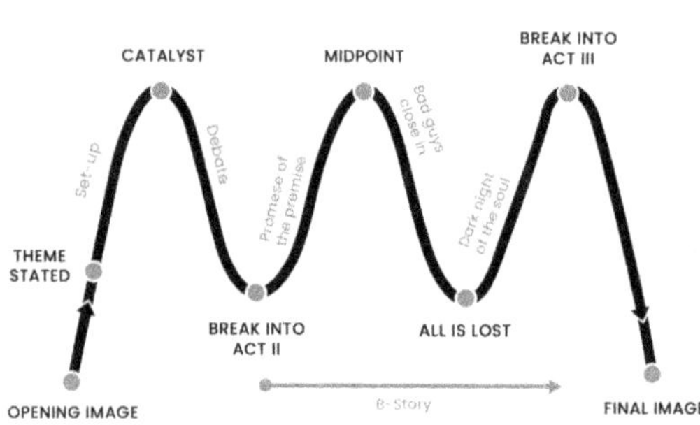

Matt Haig's *The Midnight Library* has been written using this beat sheet structure.

The narrative contains the following fifteen touchpoints:

- Opening Image—an introduction that sucks your readers into the story.
- Set-up—the readers are familiarized with the ordinary world of the protagonist, learning about what they want or are missing out on.
- Theme Stated—hints at what the story is truly about, something that the protagonist will learn about by the end.
- Catalyst—presents the inciting incident.
- Debate—the protagonist receives a call to adventure which they refuse, trying to avoid the conflict until they're forced to act.
- Break into Two—marks the conscious choice of the protagonist and the beginning of their journey. B Story—the introduction of a subplot, which is generally romantic in nature.
- Fun and Games—also referred to as the "promise of the premise" stage, is the most entertaining part of the entire story.
- Midpoint—past all the entertainment, the midpoint brings forward an unexpected plot twist that makes the protagonist's end goal difficult to achieve. Bad Guys Close In—as the protagonist's plans seem to be falling apart, the tension of the story rises incredibly.
- All Is Lost—here, the protagonist hits rock bottom, losing everything they had and being overpowered by the villain.
- Dark Night of the Soul—the protagonist is shattered and hopeless when they find a new piece of information that reveals that there might still be time for them to win.
- Break into Three—re-invigorated by their newfound hope, the protagonist is once again set on their path to victory.
- Finale—the confrontation between the protagonist and the antagonist takes place finally. The truth that was hidden from them all along is finally revealed. Final Image—the knowledge of truth brings forth changes in the protagonist's character.

G. SEVEN-POINT STORY STRUCTURE:

The seven-point story structure is developed by the author Dan Wells. Wells mentions how his structure is derived from the hero's journey narrative but is less descriptive than the latter. Suzanne Collins's *Hunger Games* series follows this narrative style.

SEVEN-POINT
STORY STRUCTURE

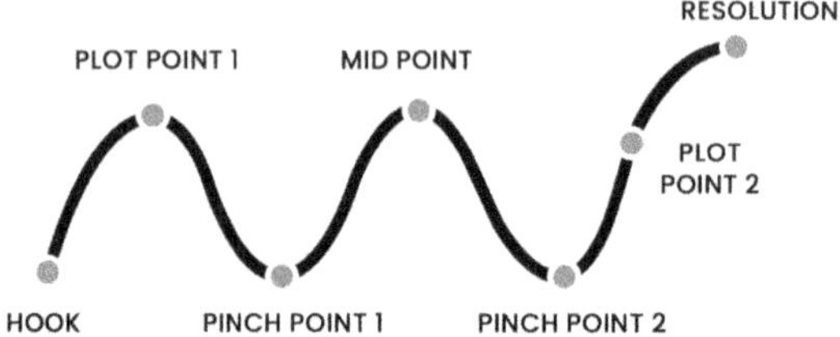

Following are the seven points of this narrative structure:

- The hook—explains to the readers the current scenario of the protagonist's life and world. The state of the world at this point is completely in contrast with that of the end.
- Plot point 1—presents a call to adventure that sets the character development and the plot in motion.
- Pinch point 1—something goes wrong in the protagonist's life that forces them to act.
- Midpoint—brings forth a turning point, where the protagonist faces the main conflict of the story.
- Pinch point 2—presents another brutal blow to the protagonist; it might also include the revelation of a betrayer or the death of a mentor.

- Plot point 2—at this point, the protagonist learns that they've had the key to solve the central conflict all along.
- Resolution—the conflict is finally resolved here, following the character development that leads to the end of the story.

These seven structure types have very similar points in them and there is a reason for that; it's because they have been tried and tested and they produce interesting likable stories. People like the ups and downs in the right places and expect things to happen a certain way. You may think that would make every story feel the same but it doesn't, the story can be different but it will only work if structured well. Think of a story like music; music uses intros, verses, a chorus, and bridges. Many songs follow the exact same structure but all songs are different; many of the same chords can be used and yet the music is diverse and still exciting to listen to. Structure is just a blueprint for a good book.

STORY ARCS:

So far, we've learned everything about story structures. Now, we'll take a quick look at story arcs. Do you know what story arcs are? Also referred to as narrative arcs, the story arcs are responsible for describing the change or shift in value in the course of a story. Simply put, these arcs provide meaning to your story.

Many writers seem to be confused between story arcs and character arcs. The best way to differentiate between the two is this: while all character arcs are story arcs, not all story arcs are character arcs. While every story must have at least one story arc, many authors often employ several story arcs in their novels as well. Emily St. John Mandel's novel *Station Eleven* is a great example of one such novel.

If you want to use story arcs in your writing, here are some quick tips that can help you in the process:

- **Ensure that your story has movement.** Any good story must have movement; otherwise, it'd simply be an account of events.

- **You needn't find the arc in the beginning.** You shouldn't stress over finding your arc from the beginning. If you have a clear idea of the plot, it shouldn't necessarily match a particular arc. **Focus on the core value.** While you write your story, it is more important to find your core value than your story arc.
- **The knowledge of your genre helps in finding your arc.** Finding a suitable arc won't be problematic for you if you know which genre your story will belong to from the beginning.
- **Build your first draft toward the dilemma.** When you're working on your first draft, make sure it's headed toward the climactic point. Don't overstuff with unimportant details.
- **Find and enhance story arcs in your second draft.** Once you're done writing the first draft, the revision process in the second one will bring you closer to finding and enhancing the story arcs.

And now, it's time for another fun exercise to nudge forward the writer within you. Here are your tasks for today:

- Out of the seven story structures we've talked about in the chapter, pick the one that appeals to you the most.
- Based on the structure, create a six-sentence story by adding one sentence for all six elements: exposition, inciting incident, rising action, crisis, climax, and resolution.
- Set an alarm for fifteen minutes. During this time, work on expanding on your six-sentence story as much as you can.

Good luck!

CHAPTER 4

CHARACTER, NOT CARICATURE

"Good characters are why most people read, I think."

This quote by Joe Bunting, a bestselling American writer, puts to words what every reader and writer thinks about the characters of their story. As a writer, one of the most important things you must know is that, while a story can be about one or many characters, without characters there can be no story.

In order to write a good story, you not only need to build characters but also make them well-developed and well-rounded. Otherwise, they will be flat and uninteresting to your readers. And, if your characters can't capture the readers' attention, you can't expect them to keep reading, can you? Come, let's learn all about the art of characterization together.

THE ART OF CHARACTERIZATION:

The art of characterization has three pillars; together, all three of these uphold the responsibility of keeping your story interesting and engaging. These are:

Physical Characterization:

As the name itself suggests, physical characterization refers to possibly minute, but unusual physical details about the characters that tend to stick with the readers, making them remember your characters distinctly. These details could even have an interesting backstory to add to your plot, such as a crooked knee, thick eyebrows, or left-handedness.

Psychological Characterization:

Psychological characterization refers to those psychological details about your characters that might not be directly relevant to the plot but help you in building their personality. It could be an unusual fear of, say, closed spaces, darkness, or even bugs. Moreover, you could also plan which of your characters are unnecessarily biased; which one tends to overthink; and which one would have dark, secret desires that could surprise the readers.

Social Circumstances:

The social circumstances of your characters also add to their character arcs, in addition to giving more authenticity to your story. These could include the details of where they grew up, which school or college they went to, where they work, their profession, and so on.

THE KIND OF CHARACTERS THAT APPEAL TO THE READERS:

It is true that the protagonists are the character on whom the entire story relies. However, if your protagonist is the only likable character in your story, your readers might find themselves getting bored of them eventually. After all, one character alone cannot hold up the whole story. That's why all great stories have more than one character that can keep the readers engaged. If you can make your readers care about characters other than the protagonist, then you can truly succeed as a writer.

But how will you achieve that? Let me tell you. There are three ways to make your readers care about your characters: when they feel sympathetic toward them, when they admire them for their virtues, and when they've found a desirable quality that they're drawn to.

Now, we'll talk about how you can use these pointers to create appealing characters in your story:

Create underdogs and victims.

As a writer, you already know how vulnerability is like a magnet for the readers. Combine vulnerability with innocence and determination, and you've found the perfect character for your story.

For your underdog character, you'll need to create a person who is weak or vulnerable because of their health, age, sex, injury, mental or emotional state. For instance, when the readers read about a young boy fighting cancer or a damsel being pursued by goons, your readers will immediately feel fiercely protective of them. They'd want them safe and happy at all costs.

However, for your readers to truly connect with these underdogs, you must bestow them with at least a couple of noble qualities like selflessness, courage, optimism, or generosity. Only then will the readers believe that this character rightfully deserves their sympathies.

Create characters that the readers can look up to.

While some readers might not feel sympathetic toward your underdogs or victims, the character I'll talk about now will certainly be well-liked by all readers equally.

This one is a decent, upright character who demonstrates all the humane qualities at their finest. Now you might wonder what's so new and refreshing about a decent, upright character? The answer is more nuanced than that.

While these characters don't bring anything new to the table, the strength of their character, their righteousness is something that can move any reader timelessly.

When you're building this character, make sure that they're the kind of person that derives joy in helping others, particularly the less fortunate. Service professions like a nurse, doctor, police officer, or teacher are most well-suited for them; take your pick.

To give these characters more depth, you can also add an instance of solitude where they reveal their true self when they think no one is looking.

Create a character who is unusual and interesting.

Do you remember when we discussed earlier that most readers read stories to escape reality? Well, in creating your unusual character, you might just be fulfilling your readers' fantasies and desires.

This unusual character shouldn't fit into any stereotypes in your story; they should be strong, independent, and incredibly attractive—both physically and mentally. A glimpse into their life should provide your readers with an experience they've never had.

The source of this character's power lies in noble birth, wealth, or sheer physical strength. To add to their charisma, give them a quality or skill that contrasts with their personality. For instance, they may be a boxer and write poetry in secret; this contradiction lends more appeal to their character.

If you can create these characters and weave them within your story, you will never have to worry about boring your readers at any point.

5 TYPES OF CHARACTERS THAT ARE MUST-HAVES IN EVERY GREAT STORY:

Did you know that there are five major characters in any story that act as pillars that uphold its plot? The first one is, without a doubt, the protagonist, while the other four include an antagonist, a mentor, a sidekick, and a skeptic.

Have you already finalized an outline with all of these characters? If not, don't worry. I'm here to help you with it. Let's get into the details:

The Protagonist:

Commonly referred to as the hero or heroine of the story, the protagonist is the central, and often the most important, character of the entire story. However, it doesn't mean that they necessarily have to be good, morally upright, or conform to any other stereotype. The only thing that you need to keep in mind while creating this character is that your readers should be able to relate to them.

As the writer, you're more likely to use their voice or perspective in your story. Therefore, whether your character makes a good or a bad decision, it is important that your readers understand it and root for them. So, when you're building your protagonist's character, make them relatable and humane and not perfect because perfection is never something your readers will look for. Provide the protagonist with both good and bad qualities, but make sure that their good qualities surpass the bad ones so that they can remain in the readers' good books in the end.

As a general rule, most works of fiction usually have a single protagonist. However, depending on the genre of your story, it might be possible to create more protagonists as well. For example, romance is a genre that has two protagonists almost all the time.

The Antagonist:

Since protagonists are referred to as the hero of the story, most people automatically assume that the antagonist would be the villain: the exact opposite of everything the protagonist stands for. But while the last part might be true, that doesn't make the antagonist purely evil.

You must remember that neither your protagonist nor antagonist can be completely good or bad. As humans, they are bound to have both good and bad qualities. But then, how are antagonists different from protagonists, or any other character in the story for that matter?

The best way to recognize an antagonist is to observe their role in the life of your protagonist. If a character is moving against the protagonist and not with them, it means that they're the antagonist.

The role of an antagonist is equally crucial in the story, as they create obstacles on the path of the protagonist. Without them, your protagonist would achieve what they're meant to in the first few pages of the story. In other words, the antagonist is as crucial to the story as the protagonist.

A common mistake that most beginner writers make while creating their antagonists is to skip giving them a realistic backstory. This makes their character very one-dimensional, and nobody wants to read about such characters. Make sure they have a fully-developed character with a justified, if not fair, motive behind their interference, interruption, or attack on the protagonist. Additionally, if you can convey to your readers that your protagonist and antagonist are not all that different, it will add more appeal to your story.

Lastly, always provide your antagonist with a certain redeeming quality that keeps your readers from hating them whole-heartedly. If your readers can feel even a shred of compassion for the antagonist, their whole reading experience becomes elevated. Some of the best stories have a protagonist and antagonist that are equally likable, which makes the final showdown even more exciting.

The Mentor:

Who is a mentor in a story? A person who is wise, righteous, and helps the protagonist achieve their destiny throughout the course of the story. In many ways, this wise guide plays an equally vital role as the protagonist, if not more. If you can make your readers feel that there would be no story without the mentor, you've succeeded in creating a great mentor character.

The character of the mentor is crucial to a story to make the protagonist seem more realistic. All of us need someone to guide us in life, don't we? If your protagonist doesn't need a guide and can do everything on their own, would they truly be realistic? Not really. It will be the mentor's job to prepare the protagonist to deal with and overcome all obstacles that come their way.

However, this doesn't mean that your mentor should be an infallible character. They must possess a flaw or weakness as well. And in most good stories, there comes a point where this flaw or weakness is exploited to attack the protagonist.

To make their character more interesting, you can withhold this flaw in the story, not sharing it with the readers until absolutely necessary.

The Sidekick:

Who is a sidekick? Most often the protagonist's sibling, cousin, friend, or colleague, the sidekick is a character that remains the loyal companion of your protagonist throughout the story. They will remain by the protagonist's side through thick and thin and will, therefore, know them better than any other character in the story.

Through the sidekick's perspective, you can present your protagonist in a different light: show their vulnerabilities and shortcomings, their failures and breaking points.

A common mistake that most writers make while creating sidekicks is to make them loyal to a fault, which takes away all their personality. You must let your sidekick doubt the protagonist's decisions at times and even argue with them when necessary. In this manner, you will lend their friendship or companionship mutual respect.

The Skeptic:

As the name itself suggests, the character of the skeptic is someone who views the entire story and its events in a different light. Just like the sidekick, the skeptic is also usually a friend of the protagonist. But unlike the former, this character doesn't develop unwavering faith in the protagonist at any point and is the symbol of apprehension, and to some extent, concern.

If the sidekick represents emotion, the skeptic will be the voice of reason and logic, both of which generally go against the protagonist at some point in the story. And while the skeptic might doubt the protagonist's choices or decisions at several points, they're not their enemy.

You must draw their character in a way that the readers are able to distinguish between the skeptic and the antagonist clearly. Because, in the end, the protagonist's victory is going to bring them joy as well.

Once you've created all these major characters successfully, the rest of the minor characters would come easily to you.

QUALITIES THAT MAKE THE PROTAGONIST STAND OUT:

So far, we've discussed how you can create a basic outline of your protagonist, who is supposed to become the most compelling character of your entire story. But once you've created an outline, how will you make them extraordinary? Well, there are many ways you can go about it. And the good news is, you can employ more than one technique to give your protagonist's character an edge.

Here are some interesting methods you can use to elevate your protagonist:

Provide your protagonist with a goal that isn't easy to achieve.

All protagonists have a certain purpose in life, a purpose that keeps the story moving. Whether it's a dream they've dreamed all their life or a goal that they absolutely have to achieve. For this, you needn't build an all-important, allconsuming goal, like saving the planet or something equally significant. The goal could be a small, generalized one, too. All you need to do is make your protagonist want it desperately enough. The importance of this goal needn't be universally crucial, only to your protagonist.

Your protagonist's goal will ultimately become the goal of your whole story, so you must choose it wisely. Go for a goal that's concrete and tangible, not something abstract that may leave the readers confused in the end.

Some interesting goal ideas you can use are:

- The resolution of a conflict with a friend, family members, community, or between two different organizations or even countries.
- Winning in an important battle or contest where the stakes are high and personal for the protagonist.
- Solving a mystery from the past. This mystery could either be from the protagonist's past or involve someone close to them.

Increase the stakes of your protagonist's goal.

Once you've provided your protagonist with a goal, you also need to justify why it is so important to them and your story. What's their motivation to pursue this goal so fiercely against all the odds you've added in the story? It is essential that you clearly define your protagonist's motivation behind achieving the goal. Moreover, you must ensure that their motivation is strong, clear, and above all, personal.

When you give the goal a personal touch, it will automatically raise the stakes for the protagonist. Additionally, a personal, preferably emotional link between the protagonist and their goal will make your readers feel more connected to your story.

Keep in mind that the higher the stakes of the goal, the more worried your readers would be about the success, or failure, of the protagonist.

Show your readers how the protagonist feels about all the events in the story.

If you've done the job of creating your protagonist well, it is possible that your readers will feel deeply connected to them and would want to learn about their feelings and thoughts about all the ups and downs of the story. And to satisfy your readers, you must give them a peek into the protagonist's thoughts about all these happenings.

When your readers share in both the joys and the torments of the protagonist alike, their empathy for them will grow considerably. In this manner, they will soon start seeing themselves in the shoes of your protagonist, which is exactly what you should aim for.

How you shape your protagonist's past is crucial.

From the beginning of your story, your readers are walking alongside the protagonist, experiencing everything together. But what about their past? If your story doesn't begin right from the birth of the protagonist, they'd certainly want to learn about how their life was before the story began.

Now, you could make their past a simple, uneventful one, but where's the fun in that? To make these characters stand out, you should give them a past that has had a deep impact on their psyche, some troubling or disturbing event that altered their lives forever.

For instance, in the Harry Potter series, the past of Harry was tragic because of the fact that Lord Voldemort brutally killed his parents when he was an infant. This incident changed Harry's life forever, forcing him to live with his cruel aunt and uncle in a world of muggles until he was eleven years old. His mean-spirited aunt and uncle probably helped him become a better person simply by exposing him to the ugliness of their family and making him want to be different from them.

If you can give your protagonist a past like that, you can also show how it has shaped them as a person. They could have insecurities, fear of intimacy, or become embittered toward everything.

Does your protagonist have a tragic flaw?

As we discussed earlier, no reader enjoys reading about a protagonist who is perfect. And while adding some minor flaws to their character is all right, it is vital to provide them with a tragic flaw. You must give them an iconic flaw that might bring them down to their lowest point later in the story. And this flaw should be presented to the readers early in the story itself. If it comes as a surprise to them, they will find it hard to believe and might become disconnected from the character altogether. Let's use *Back to the Future* as an example. Marty McFly won't allow anyone to call him "chicken." Throughout the three movies, it is the one comment that gets him into a lot of trouble—especially with Biff Tannen—but in the end, he refuses to fire in a gunfight even though he was called yellow. He finally learns his lesson.

QUALITIES THAT MAKE THE ANTAGONIST STAND OUT:

Just like your protagonist, your antagonist is also an important character and must stand out. As you might have noticed, in every great story, both the hero and the villain have equally strong characters. Take Batman and the Joker, for instance.

Here are a few details that you can use to add depth to the character of your antagonist:

- First and foremost, you must make sure that your antagonist is a self-righteous person. Whatever others might think of them, they should believe they are heroic and justified in their motivations and actions. Even if this is just inside their heads.

- Although it goes without saying, the protagonist and antagonist shouldn't be complete strangers to each other. The more they're connected, the more interesting their enmity becomes. If they've had a troubling history or grounds for conflict, it will elevate the thrill of the entire story. It's not always possible but if you can produce a link between them, it grows the conflict.

- Make sure that your antagonist is, in every way, a worthy opponent for your protagonist. If they aren't strong enough for the protagonist, either mentally or physically, the final fight, battle, contest, or war between them wouldn't be fair. And since this conflict is the climax of the whole story, you must make it worth their while.

- All antagonists are bound to have flaws. But if you want their character to stand out, give them flaws that your readers can relate to. Because, if they relate to the antagonist's flaws, they will feel at least a shred of sympathy for them, which is the recipe of every good story.

- If the backstory of the protagonist is important, the antagonist's backstory is paramount. Your readers are bound to like the protagonist, but in order to understand the antagonist better, they must have a better understanding of their life and past experiences—everything that has played a role in shaping their personality.

- Make sure you give one charming quality to your antagonist. It is this quality, more than anything else, that will endear them to your readers no matter how hard they try to hate them. Even showing the antagonist caring for an animal will go a long way to making them charming. In most stories, the antagonists are witty or have an incredible sense of humor; you could also incorporate these qualities in yours.

By now, you will be well on your way to creating compelling characters that will add to the essence of your story. As always, it's exercise time now.

The first task that I have for you is quite simple. If you've already created a basic story structure in the last exercise, here are some questions that I want you to ponder:

- Who is the hero of this story?
- What is the major flaw or problem they're dealing with?
- Is this problem affecting their world or life? If yes, in what way?
- What's the root cause of this problem?
- What does your hero want to achieve in life? And why haven't they achieved it yet?

Here are some more writing prompts for you:

- Think about the favorite media of your protagonist: their favorite book, movie, game, or sport. These points will not only add depth to their character but also help you in making them stand out.
- Write a short story about these characters at a different age, preferably in the past. This will help you build their backstory.
- Draw a rough sketch of how you want your protagonist to look. Take care of minor details such as eye color, skin complexion, body language. These details will come in handy when you create their picture for your readers.
- Develop your protagonist's character arc beyond the plotline. It will give you a better idea of how your narrative will proceed and from where it will draw motivation.

Once you've finished these assignments, we'll move on with our next topic, where I'll tell you more about characterbuilding.

CHAPTER 5

CREATING YOUR CHARACTER

In the last chapter, we covered all the basics of what the characters of your story are supposed to look like. Now, we will learn how you can build characters who will keep your readers glued to the pages of your story.

I agree that all story elements, such as a plot, structure, and theme, are equally important. However, your characters are the ones who ultimately put life into your story. To make it clearer, let's take an example. Have you ever read a story or watched a movie that had a slightly boring or complicated plotline, but its characters were so striking that they left a lasting impression on you? That's the magic a good character can weave into your story.

Do you want your story to have such magical characters as well? Then what are we waiting for? Let's get started!

HOW TO BUILD A CHARACTER:

When you're creating your characters, you must first think about how you want to shape them. The easiest and my personal favorite way to do this is to ask and answer these five questions about them.

Question #1: Who is your protagonist? (Types, values, traits, and flaws.)

First things first, you'll need to choose what personality type you aim to lend your protagonist. You have four choices:

The Hero:

a confident, self-assured character who is always superior to the readers; someone they look up to or fantasize about, like Sherlock Holmes.

The Underdog:

a character inferior to the readers; someone who is outmatched by the villain and barely deserves to be a hero. Such a character generates protective and compassionate feelings in the readers, such as Frodo Baggins from *The Lord of the Rings*.

Mr. Average:

a regular character that readers can identify with; someone who struggles with doubts just as we do but ends up overcoming all challenges. John McClane's character in *Die Hard* is a perfect example of a Mr. Average.

The Dark Soul:

a character with a broken moral compass; someone who has embraced the dark side of human nature. While the readers might not like their character initially, over the course of the story, they will develop feelings of guilty admiration for them. The character of the Godfather in the namesake movie represents the dark soul beautifully.

Once you've chosen which personality type you want to go with, it's time to select their values. All protagonists should have beliefs, passions, and views that are unique to them alone. These values will set them apart from the other characters of your story until the very end.

To provide more depth to your character, you should also give them quirky traits: something that they like, dislike, or a skill they've mastered. Your readers shouldn't expect these traits about your character initially but will grow to love them eventually.

Lastly, you need to decide what would be your character's major flaw. As humans, all of us are bound to have some flaw, which is why it will add a humane touch to your protagonist. This flaw could stem from the fears, resentments, or emotional damage in their past.

As soon as you've made all these choices, you can proceed to the second question.

Question #2: What do they want? (Their goals and desires.)

Your story's ultimate climax comes from the protagonist's main goal or desire, which is why it serves as the backbone of the entire story. It could be resolving a personal conflict, saving one's family or nation, or making a difficult decision. Your protagonist can have multiple goals as well, but one of them will certainly dominate all others.

Question #3: Why do they want it? (Motivation behind seeking their goal.)

Would you still be getting up early in the morning if you didn't have to go to work? Perhaps not. All of our actions have some motivation or another, and the same is true for your protagonist. If they want something that badly, there must be a compelling reason or need behind it. This motivation is the driving factor in your plot, so you better choose it wisely.

Question #4: What happens if they fail to achieve it? (High stakes.)

All good stories have exceptionally high stakes, which keeps the readers on edge the entire time. Whatever your protagonist is aiming for, you must tell your readers the consequences if they fail to achieve it. And these consequences should be severe, almost life-threatening. It will drive the readers to root for their success wholeheartedly, making them care more about the story in the process.

Question #5: Do they change throughout the course of the story? If so, how? (Character arc.)

The answer to this question often lies in the personality type that you've chosen for your protagonist. Not all protagonists need to change in the course of the story. However, if you want your story to be more compelling, go for this change. Also, describe to your readers elaborately why the change was necessary and what its consequences are in the end.

BUILDING MULTI-LAYERED CHARACTERS:

There are two ways in which you can write your story. The first one is a plot-driven story, and the second one is a character-driven story. If you're planning to go with the latter, it is essential that your characters have multiple layers; these layers could consist of several sides to their personalities, each linked to some experience in the past.

The secret to successfully creating multi-layered characters lies in revealing each layer slowly so that the suspense remains intact. If you unload all the layers on your readers at once, they will feel over-whelmed and might not want to continue reading. Always remember that there's a right time for everything, and you'll be fine.

HOW CAN YOU KEEP YOUR READERS INVESTED IN YOUR CHARACTERS:

As a writer, you all must know that your readers will form a bond with the characters in your story as soon as they meet them (or read about them). However, if you want that bond to grow stronger throughout the course of your story, here are three ways you can make that happen:

Recognition:

You must provide the readers with a deeper understanding of your characters. Talk about their sorrowful or difficult past. This will not only make your characters full but also help in making the readers sympathize with them continually.

While you're on it, add some emotion-provoking details to their backstory that will compel the readers to relate to your characters and feel what they might be feeling. This can be done by highlighting the inner conflicts of your characters: their guilt, remorse, and doubts.

Fascination:

All readers are attracted to characters that are different in some way or another. But how can you make your characters remarkably different? There are many ways to go about it:

Give your characters a unique personality; quirky traits; strong, individual beliefs and attributes. Make them seem more like a real person.

Make your characters care about things that all readers can relate to: family, love, freedom, and so on.

Always, always be careful while building their backstories. These are what truly connect the readers with your characters.

Mystery:

By mystery, I mean it in an emotional sense. Make your characters capable of surprising the readers at every step so that they will never know what's going to hit them next.

MAKING YOUR PROTAGONISTS COMPELLING:

Considering the fact that your protagonist is central to your whole story, you must always strive to add more gravitas to their character. Here are some pointers that can help you in making your characters more compelling:

- **Is your protagonist's goal easily achievable?** The central goal of your protagonist is what you build your climax on. Therefore, if it isn't thrilling enough, your readers will end up feeling disappointed. To add another twist to the tale, you can give the protagonist a false goal in the beginning and reveal their true goal much later in the story.
- **The strengths of your protagonist should be clearly defined.** By strength, I do not mean a supernatural skill or quality, just basic positive traits like high morality, determination, and so on. While your protagonist must have some flaws, make sure that their strengths overpower them significantly.
- **Raise the stakes of the story gradually.** While all readers like a good climax in the story, you have to make sure it is believable and realistic as well. If you've set the bar too high from the

beginning and your protagonist still manages to achieve it somehow, it will make their character seem unrealistic to your readers. Instead, go slow and build the suspense gradually.

- **The past of your protagonist is as essential as their present.** You must have heard the saying, "You are what you've been through." Therefore, you should create your protagonist's story very carefully and intricately. The events of their past must reflect how their personalities have been formed.

- **Does your protagonist have a dark nature?**Remember the Dark Soul personality we discussed earlier? Well, if you've chosen that personality for your character, you must have to balance it out by showing your readers a glimpse of their good side as well. And how would you go about it? There are several methods you can adopt to achieve this. Add small acts of kindness or selflessness to the story that will earn your protagonist a soft corner in the readers' hearts.

Put them in contrast with other, worse characters, or even the antagonist. Lastly, give your readers a sense of hope that no matter how dark, these characters can also be redeemed. But if you adopt this last method, make sure not to leave them hanging in the end. Your protagonist should ultimately be redeemed.

CREATING AN UNFORGETTABLE VILLAIN/ANTAGONIST:

If your protagonist is the backbone of your story, the antagonist or villain is its legs. Therefore, you cannot undermine their importance under any circumstances. If you're looking for ways to create an antagonist that your readers will never forget, here are some pointers:

- **Draw inspiration from real people.** While it is easy to build a protagonist solely out of imagination, the antagonist's character often needs more motivation than that. Therefore, it is always best to look for inspiration from someone you know, either personally or through a book, movie, play, or other fictional works. Most of us have met unpleasant people in our lives, people who are bad-mannered, impatient, selfish, or just plain rude. You could sprinkle some of their characteristics into the antagonist and then balance it out with, perhaps, a love of animals or a fondness of children. You really can create any combination as long as it's believable to the reader.

- **Put yourself in the shoes of your antagonist.** No matter how unjust or cruel your antagonist is, they're still people with at least some shred of humanity, right? Try to think of events or circumstances that can potentially bring out your worst self and compel you to react harshly. These events can contribute to building a realistic backstory for your villain.
- **Bring your antagonist into the story with a bang.** The antagonist is not like the characters that your readers can gradually learn about. In the case of this character, you have to make their intentions clear from the very beginning. And the best way to do that is to plan their entrance in a strong, definitive manner.

- **Can your readers sympathize with your antagonist?** Many writers seem to think that in a good story, the readers should ideally love the protagonist and hate the antagonist. But that's not true. As humans, we are subconsciously looking for the hope that we can all be redeemed despite our flaws and wrongdoings. If your antagonist has that quality as well, it'll be easier for your readers to connect with them.
- **Highlight the similarities between the protagonist and antagonist.** All of us have a good and a bad side to ourselves, don't we? If you can present that idea between your protagonist and antagonist, it's going to make your story much more interesting for the readers.

With this, we come to the end of this chapter. But before turning the page over to the next chapter, I have two interesting activities to brush up on your writing skills.

- Write a one-page character description. If you've completed the activity at the end of the last chapter, it's time for you to elaborate on that. Pick one of these characters and think about what kind of person you want them to be. Start jotting your thoughts down, and don't stop until you're at the end of the page.

- Create interior monologues. Pick a character; it can either be the one you used in the last activity or a new character altogether. Now, start writing a onepage monologue about what they could be thinking or feeling at any given part of the story. This exercise can be completed more efficiently while sitting in a park or garden, where you can see several people engaged in different activities. You can find your motivation more easily in such places.

Have fun with these activities, and we shall meet again for the next chapter.

CHAPTER 6
YOUR CHARACTER'S JOURNEY

In the last chapter, we learned how characters put life into your story. But have you ever wondered what kind of characters can successfully attract most readers to your story? Characters who are capable of evolving throughout the course of the story.

Let me show you with the help of an example. When you were ten years old, you must have had a very different and childish mindset, right? And at that time, it was completely all right. However, if you had the same mindset now that you're an adult and living independently, would it help you? Certainly not. While playing hide-and-seek outside with your friends all day long seems acceptable at the age of ten, could you still do it at the age of thirty? You could, but I think the neighbors might worry about you.

This is just one instance of how different stages of life demand a different version of you. And what would help you achieve it? Change and evolution. When we learn from our experiences, we grow in life. And as a writer, you must show your characters' growth to your readers so that they can see them as real people and not merely as fictional characters.

In other words, if you wish to create good stories, working on your character development alone isn't going to help you. You will have to employ character arcs as well. But what do these arcs mean? Let's find out.

WHAT ARE CHARACTER ARCS:

Many people tend to confuse story arcs and character arcs, although they're two completely separate things. While the plot is a series of events that together build your story, the character arc is a series of events that build your character. These events throw light on each character's internal struggles and conflicts and show your readers how the character has grown through them.

In other words, your character arc will tell the story of how the character began and how they ended up in the story. Now, it is not always necessary for these characters to undergo a major change in the story; they can remain the same person in the end, too. All you need to ensure is that they undertake a journey, be it physical, spiritual, or emotional, and they grow through it, with your readers growing alongside them.

Are you still feeling confused between the story arc and character arc? Let me take the example of the Harry Potter series to clarify your concerns. In the series, the story arc is how Harry is raised at Hogwarts to ultimately fight the last battle with Lord Voldemort. On the other hand, Harry's character arc shows how he learns and changes through all his experiences at Hogwarts and grows in confidence and determination to be one of the best wizards the world has seen. While there's a close connection between the story arc and the character arc here, they're still significantly different.

Before we delve deeper into character arcs, let's quickly look at three categories, which can be broadly categorized as:

Change Arc:

Most commonly seen in all good stories, the change arc follows an ordinary, underdog-like character that ultimately ends up achieving large goals like saving or protecting their worlds, planets, countries, or communities.

The character arc of Katniss Everdeen in *The Hunger Games* is a perfect example of a change arc.

Growth Arc:

Although the growth arc is somewhat similar to the change arc, it has a more subtle tone. The character around which this arc revolves doesn't undergo a drastic change or impact the lives of millions. They mostly change themselves for the better without changing the world.

Their struggle is more personal in nature and changes them in a very limited sense by the end of the story.

For instance, take Elizabeth Bennet from *Pride and Prejudice*. By the end of the novel, Lizzie retains all the values and qualities that she had from the beginning. Only her views about prejudice and pride change throughout the course of the story.

Fall Arc:

Distinguished from the first two arcs, the fall arc works in a different direction altogether. As the name itself suggests, it shows the downfall of the character. The character that goes through this arc is wealthy and successful in the beginning and ends up losing everything they held dear by the end.

The transition of Anakin Skywalker's character into Darth Vader in the *Star Wars* movies is a perfect example of the fall arc.

WHY DO YOU NEED CHARACTER ARCS:

Now that we've learned what character arcs are, how many of you can tell me why they're so crucial to your story? There are three main reasons why your story absolutely needs character arcs:

- **Character arcs add emotional weight to your story.** Suppose that you only get to see what happens to a character in the story and not how it makes them feel. Will you be able to relate to them? No. In order to relate to someone, we must know something personal about them; understand their struggles, joys, fears, and dreams.If you can show these features of your character, your readers will grow to care about them deeply, as if they knew them personally.

- **Character arcs lend a certain depth to the character.** Have you ever noticed how we grow more attached to the protagonist of a story than other side characters? This is because we know the former more intimately than any other character, which makes us identify with their thoughts and beliefs.

- **Character arcs are often the foundation of a story's themes.** What is the theme of your story? Is it love, friendship, family, or something else? Whatever it is, you can highlight it more conveniently by weaving it into your protagonist's character arc. Because when your protagonist learns something, your readers learn it alongside them.It is because character arcs can do all these things for your story that they're absolutely necessary. While a story can survive without these arcs as well, if you want your story to stand out, you'll have to take the pain of developing them. Now, let me tell you how you can create these arcs.

CREATING CHARACTER ARCS:

If you feel like creating character arcs is complicated, you are mistaken. It's barely any different from character development. Remember how you formed a basic outline of your characters in the last chapter? Well, here, you will add more depth to their characters.

Let's begin by covering the basics. Whenever I need to create a character arc for my story, I start with answering these four questions about the character being considered:

Question #1: Who is the character?

Think about what you want your character to be like at the beginning of the story. What are their interests, thoughts, beliefs, and principles? What makes their character important to the story? All these details will help you develop their character.

Question #2: How and why do they start their journey?

All great journeys have a strong motivation behind them. What's your character's motivation for moving forward in the story? Are they unhappy with their current circumstances? Or is there an external force nudging them into taking action? Their motive for the entire journey must be clarified at the beginning itself, otherwise, their character will appear flat and boring.

Question #3: What are the obstacles on their path?

Once your character has set out on their journey, the obstacles they will face are the whole plot of the story. If obtaining their end goal were that easy, you'd be wrapping up the story in a couple of pages.

The challenges faced by your characters are generally of two types: personal (or internal) and external. The personal challenges include their own flaws or shortcomings that keep them from achieving their goals. On the other hand, the external obstacles are factors that they've no control over.

Question #4: How will they change?

If you've found the answer to the first three questions, it will lead you to your fourth question. The change in their character often arises from necessity; it could be something they need to do in order to achieve their final goal.

Another interesting way of creating character arcs is by dividing their growth and development into six different stages:

Stage 1: In the first stage, you will show your character in their full persona. It will contain a detailed description of what they look like to the outer world.

Stage 2: In the second stage, the character will experience an opposing external force. Perhaps their beliefs or principles are being questioned, and they get an idea of what they could be if they changed their ideology.

Stage 3: The third stage shows the character embarking on their journey. And while they're essentially the same person, you can notice a gradual change in their character if you observe them closely.

Stage 4: The fourth stage is where your character will reach the realization that they need to change themselves in order to achieve their goals. They have learned that by not embracing their true self, they're failing themselves as well as their loved ones.

Stage 5: The fifth stage comes with the arrival of the central climax. In this stage, your character will fully embrace their true self. They will face a challenge that puts everything at stake. Despite being afraid, they will still take it on, giving it their best.

Stage 6: The sixth stage comes with the resolution of the plot. After overcoming the climax, your character has evolved into a different person. They now have a healthier relationship with themselves.

CREATING POSITIVE CHARACTER ARCS:

All good stories have a stellar positive character arc because, in fiction, a happy ending is what all readers generally seek. We see a character struggling with a major internal conflict and ultimately overcoming it in these character arcs.

When you're creating a positive character arc, the first thing you need to do is to establish a lie. Your characters have been telling themselves this lie all their lives. However, during the course of the story, they're faced with the truth that counters their lie. The truth then leads their character to transform into a better version of themselves.

For instance, your character might believe that they're unworthy of love due to all the bad deeds they've committed in life, which is the lie here. And the truth is that despite all their wrongdoings, they're still human beings who deserve to be loved.

You can also add instances where the readers realize how living a lie is hurting the character and their loved ones for more depth and clarity.

CREATING NEGATIVE CHARACTER ARCS:

Just like positive character arcs, negative character arcs are also involved in a tug-of-war between lie and truth. There are three types of arcs that these characters can follow:

Disillusionment Arc:

In this arc, the character overcomes the lie and learns the truth, ultimately. However, they find the truth to be far too tragic. In conclusion: They don't like the truth.

Corruption Arc:

In this arc, the truth is in front of the character throughout the story, but they choose to ignore it and embrace the lie they've been living in. They desire the lie more than the truth. In conclusion: They love the lie.

Fall Arc:

In this arc, the character is in the presence of a positive truth the entire time, but they continue to drown in sorrow and misery because the lie is an obstacle they can't overcome. In conclusion: It's impossible to get to the truth.

When you're creating a negative character arc, these pointers might help you a great deal. They sure helped me. Take a look:

- Recognize the major flaw in your character, which will ultimately lead them to their downfall in the story. It could be greed, ego, insecurity, or any number of things.
- Clearly define the belief that you will use as the foundation of their lie and truth.
- Gradually develop the strong motivation that pushes them to act against the positive characters in the story.
- Answer these five questions about them: What are their personal values and moral beliefs in life?
- Do they have a clearly defined boundary that they'd never cross in life?
- What can push them off their moral ledge?
- If they fail to overcome their lie or accept their truth, what might they face?
- What effects do their limiting beliefs have on the people around them?

CREATING STATIC CHARACTER ARCS:

While the positive and negative character arcs depict the struggle and internal conflict of characters that help them evolve throughout the course of the story, static character arcs are for the flat characters of your story.

Therefore, their character arc revolves around holding to their core values despite the odds of the story. The end purpose of these characters is not to change themselves but to change the world around them in small ways or big ways.

The main reason behind these characters being called static is that they possess a strong sense of identity throughout the entire story; there's no lie that they struggle with, only truth.

And when you're creating their character arcs, here are the things you need to do:

- Because their personal beliefs and identity are most important to these characters, you should start by defining them.
- These characters must have a truth that they hold very dear. You need to define it clearly.
- In order to add some obstacles to their path, you can also give them some temptations that might make their purpose dwindle along the way.

Answer the following questions about these characters:

- Who or what will challenge their truth?
- What lie do they want your character to believe to corrupt them? And how will it benefit them? Could following this lie bring forward a conflict between them and the antagonist?
- What are the stakes for the static character?
- What can push them to their breaking point?

Once you have answers to all these questions, you can easily create a detailed character arc for this static character.

MAPPING THE KEY MOMENTS:

Do you remember how we talked about different plot points of your story earlier in the book? Well, now that you've learned all about character arcs, you will need to fill in their beats at every plot point to create a road map for your writing. Let's begin:

#1: The Hook

POSITIVE: Showcase your character within their everyday environment, introduce their lie, and depict how it affects their daily life.

NEGATIVE: Introduce your character to their everyday world. In disillusionment or fall arcs, bring forth their lie and show how it impacts their world. In the corruption arc, introduce their truth instead.

STATIC: Depict the everyday life of your character. Show how they accept their truth, favoring it over the lie.

#2: The Inciting Incident

POSITIVE: Bring in some unprecedented events that trigger a change in your character's everyday life. These events can either reveal a part of their truth or challenge the lie they're living.

NEGATIVE: Introduce some unexpected events that provide them a chance to reaffirm their lie.

STATIC: Introduce unforeseen events that might catch these characters off-guard, threatening their truth or introducing a temptation. These characters will react to the situation by trying to escape it.

#3: First Plot Point

POSITIVE: Another series of unexpected events that pushes them irreversibly to accept the changes they must undergo. A glimpse of them setting out on their journey.

NEGATIVE: Set them out on a journey unconsciously; a journey that will ultimately lead to their downfall.

STATIC: Another unexpected event that your characters cannot run from. With this event, they're forced to acknowledge their world must be changed and pursue a means to preserve their truth. **#4: Series of Events**

POSITIVE: A series of defensive conflicts. All the conflicts your character now faces will aim to highlight the flaws of the lie they live in.

NEGATIVE: A series of discomforting events. Whether your character holds their truth or lie firmly, these events will shake their foundation.

STATIC: A series of unsettling events. Your characters will be overpowered by the obstacles thrown their way because they lack the complete knowledge about this journey they've undertaken.

#5: The Midpoint

POSITIVE: Introduce a major conflict that will force your character to confront their truth.

NEGATIVE: Bring your character face to face with their truth or lie, either of which will push them into an irreversible action.

STATIC: While your character has been fighting for the truth so far, they now realize that it would be easier to just accept the lie.

#6: Series of Events

POSITIVE: A series of transformative events. Your character will go through a series of events that will show them how they can benefit if they stop running from their truth and accept it.

NEGATIVE: A series of devolving events. Once your character has committed the irreversible action, the next series of events will give them an idea of how their downfall is underway.

STATIC: A series of empowering conflicts. These events strengthen your character to participate actively in the pursuit of their goals.

#7: Turning Point

POSITIVE: A false victory. On the transformative path, your character is about to achieve the goal associated with their lie. They choose to fulfill their goal, which will lead to a false victory.

NEGATIVE: A tragic realization. Now that your character already has an idea about what's to come, a devastating event makes it all the more transparent for them.

STATIC: The dark night of the soul. While your character is set on their path, an unexpected event occurs, threatening to harm them or their loved ones.

#8: Third Plot Point

POSITIVE: While your character might believe that they've chosen the right path, they really haven't. Very soon, the realization of its falsity will dawn on them, pushing them to ultimately give up their lie.

NEGATIVE: The tragedy that befell your character earlier has rendered them helpless.

STATIC: After the tragic events that took place earlier, something else happens that reignites their hope.

#9: Climactic Sequence

POSITIVE: The central conflict of your character's life will be resolved.

NEGATIVE: Your character will experience their last tragedy unfolding in front of them.

STATIC: A confrontation between your character's truth and the antagonist's lie takes place.

#10: Resolution

POSITIVE: Your character has finally accepted their truth and makes amends for the damage they've caused under the influence of their lie.

NEGATIVE: Your character cannot do much to resolve their tragic downfall, and their character arc comes to a close.

STATIC: Your character wins their battle and is successful in transforming the world around them for the better.

With this, we're at the end of this chapter. I've told you everything you need to know about character arcs, which means you're now ready to practice writing them by yourself. Here's an exercise to help you work on it.

In order to create a character arc successfully, you need to be familiar with your character: learn about their strengths, weaknesses, beliefs, and more. Here's how you can do it:

Pick a character you've created and place them in diverse scenarios to see how they'd react to them. Here are some possible scenarios you can use:

- Your character is getting drinks after work when a fistfight starts right next to them.
- Their partner chooses to break up with them over texts.
- They lied on their resume to get a job and are now nervous about the interview.
- They are at the hospital, receiving a distressing prognosis.
- A relative, someone they tend to avoid, has come to visit and has some news for them.
- A scenario in which they are scared to death and how they handle it.
- A scenario where they're required to make a tough decision.
- A scenario where they have to break difficult news to someone.
- A scenario where they wake up in the body of someone else.
- A scenario where they apologize to someone and it blows up in their face.

I hope you enjoy yourself while thinking about these options. See you in the next chapter!

CHAPTER 7
COMBINING THE LOT

So far, I'm sure you've learned many new and exciting things about how to write a story that will benefit your readers. But what's the most important lesson you've learned? If you ask me, I believe that the most important thing one should learn before writing stories is that both characters and plot play equally important roles in storytelling.

Some writers tend to focus more on the plot, while others invest more effort in designing their characters. But the truth is, both of these elements require the same amount of your time and effort if your story is to be extraordinary. Let me explain it with an example.

As a reader, you must've come across a story at some point in your life that had mediocre characters but a mindblowing plot or a boring story-line with characters who left a mark on you. While both these stories might have been enjoyable to you, can you really call either one your favorite? Perhaps not. But have you wondered what went wrong in those stories? In most of these cases, the writer's mistake was not being able to combine these elements in synchrony.

Many of you might wonder why combining these elements is so complicated. But the truth is, the combination of plot and characters of a story is an art only few can master. And those few are the kind of writers all readers and writers look up to. Are you ready to learn this art? Let's begin!

COMBINING THE CHARACTERS AND PLOT:

Once you've come up with the idea for a story, you start getting into the details of it and thinking about how you will figure out elements such as plot and characters. Now, you can't come up with both these elements at once; it is possible that you will have a better structure for one of these first.

Is it the plot? Or the characters? Whichever element has a stronger foundation, in the beginning, will become the deciding factor in the whole combining process. We will start with outlining these elements, so take your pick and let's move ahead. I'm going to start with the characters; you can go with either.

Outlining the Characters:

If you're starting with your characters, I'll assume that you already have an idea about what you want the initial character to be like. Now, when you start creating their outline, the first question you need to answer is whether this character is a protagonist or an antagonist.

I know many of you believe that the first character that a writer thinks of would obviously be the protagonist of their story. But I can tell you from experience that it's not always the case. I've seen many instances wherein a writer picks up the personality traits of the antagonist first and then creates the protagonist as their counter-personality. I myself have done that in many of my short stories.

Anyhow, once you've decided whether your character will be a protag-onist or an antagonist, you can proceed to expand their personality. While you've already figured out some of their basic traits and flaws, in order to make them seem like real people and not merely flat charac-ters, you have to give them something more.

Some writers prefer to do that by making lists of their character's physical features (their eyes, lips, complexion, hair, height, physique, and so on) and their favorites (book, color, movie, city, game, music, and so on). However, in my opinion, the best way to go about it is by putting your character in different scenarios and figuring out how they will react to them. If you scroll up to the last chapter, you'll find several suggestions for these scenarios in its exercise. These scenarios do not have to be restricted to the plotline of your story; they can be outside of it, too. You need to understand that the idea here is to know more about your character's personality, not to gather more information for your story.

If you're looking to add more depth to your character's outline, you can do it by figuring out how they will interact with the other characters of the story. In this process, you will not only learn more about your character but also start developing other major and minor characters for your story. And in the end, these characters will make your story seem more lifelike.

Outlining the Plot:

If you've already found an idea for the plot of your story, you can move ahead to create an outline for it. But how would you go about it? Don't worry; I'm here to help you with it.

Whenever I create an outline for the plot of my story, the first thing I do is to figure out what category or genre my idea will be well-suited for. There are seven basic story types that I generally pick from, and so can you. We've already discussed them earlier in the book, but here's the list to jog your memory:

- Comedy
- Tragedy
- Quest
- Rags to Riches
- Rebirth
- Voyage and Return
- Overcoming a Threat

Once you've found the right category for your plot, proceed to the next step, where you will write down your idea and figure out if it's going to be the beginning, middle, or end of your story. Not all writers begin with the beginning; many will think of the ending first and then build the story around it. Some even choose the climactic point right from the start and construct the plot around it. Figuring it out will give you a nudge toward designing your plotline.

The next step in this process will involve where your characters are going to fit within this plotline, and if you've already outlined your characters, it's time for you to move to the combination process.

Combining the Two to Create an Outline:

Now that you've come this far, I'm assuming that you're already done with creating outlines for your plot and characters. So, what you have with you right now is a basic plotline along with several characters to place within it. The best way to proceed is to place your characters against the plot you've outlined and see how well they fit. Is your protagonist or antagonist a perfect fit for the plotline you've designed? Even if they aren't, or you feel like something is missing, don't worry. Remember that, even at this point, you're still constructing your outline. There are bound to be a lot of changes throughout this process. You can make as many changes and alterations in your characters and plots as you need.

If your characters fit right into the story, you can start producing scenes revolving around the characters and see how they turn out. These scenes will ultimately become events within your story. In this process, you will also lend an individual touch to your characters, ultimately developing their personalities.

As the complexity of your characters grows, the complexity of the entire plot will also deepen. As you continue, you will soon observe several subplots growing out of your basic outline. However, you cannot expect all this to happen to you in your first attempt. If it were that easy, everybody would be a writer, wouldn't they?

But unfortunately, there are no shortcuts around it. It is something that is likely to grow easier only with time and practice; the more you write, the easier you will find the process.

THE SNOWFLAKE METHOD:

Have you heard of the snowflake method of writing? This technique was devised by the award-winning novelist Randy Ingermanson, who is also popularly known as the Snowflake Guy.

While Randy designed this technique keeping novel-writing in mind, it can also prove beneficial for short stories. It basically tells you how you can create a story from scratch following five steps. The main advantage of this technique is that it provides you a middle ground between conforming to traditional outlines and writing in freestyle. If you're a writer who struggles to follow the well-established, traditional methods and techniques of story writing, the snowflake method can do wonders for you.

As I mentioned earlier, this method has five steps. Take a look at these steps below:

Step 1: Choose the basic premise from the idea you've found, and use it to write a one-sentence summary. This single sentence will end up becoming the summary of your entire story.

Step 2: Now that you have your one-lined story, you can expand that sentence into a complete paragraph. This paragraph should ideally convey the whole story in a concise manner. Following are the major elements your paragraph should include:

- It should introduce the characters that are central to your story.
- It should divide the structure of your narrative into a beginning, a middle, and an end.
- Alternatively, you can also include the exposition, the inciting incident, and the climax.
- If you want to add more than three plot points to it, feel free to do so.

Step 3: Now that you have a basic summary of the plot of your story, you can proceed to create similar summaries for your characters as well. You can start by doing it for your protagonist and antagonist and then move on to other characters that are important to the plot.

These summaries needn't extend too long. Basically, they just need to answer three main questions:

- What are the core values, beliefs, and ethics of this character?
- What is their perspective in relation to your story?
- What role will they be playing in the central plot of your story?

Step 4: The next level of your snowflake construction will require you to add to the summarized character paragraphs that you created in the last step.

Now that you have the basic structure, expanding on it should not be that difficult. In this detailed profile, you can add more to your characters. Here are some of my suggestions that you can employ for doing it:

- What is this character's name?
- What do they look like?
- What do they enjoy?
- Will they be a leading or a side character in your story?
- What is the story of their life? Past and present included.
- What are their goals?
- What are the obstacles that are standing in the way of them achieving those goals?
- Which epiphany will help them overcome these obstacles and achieve their goals?

Step 5: This is the final step of the snowflake method. So far, you've already created a core story; a basic, multi-part structure of the plot; and the names and profiles of multiple characters. What's the next step? It is writing a brief synopsis using these materials. Your synopsis will ideally range between four and five pages in length. In it, you will talk about all the major events and the characters that will be involved in them. Lastly, you will also expand on the climactic point of your story here because it is, after all, what your whole story relies on.

Once you've gone through all these steps and have the synopsis prepared, you are ready to dive into fully-fledged writing. In the next chapter, I'll discuss everything you need to know about creating the supporting characters for your story.

CHAPTER 8
SUPPORTING CHARACTERS

A good story has an extraordinary protagonist; a great story has an extraordinary protagonist and antagonist; but an outstanding story has an extraordinary protagonist, antagonist, and at least one supporting character.

As John Donne wrote, "No man is an island." As strong or independent as someone may be, they will still need people in their lives: people to learn from; rely on; and share their joys, sorrows, and troubles with. After all, there's a good reason why we humans are considered social animals.

As a writer, if you're hoping to write a story that your readers can connect to, you must try to make it as close to reality as possible. And the best way to do that is to show your readers how your protagonist also needs someone they can count on. This is exactly the kind of thing you need a supporting character for. They will either help or encourage your protagonist; challenge them to become stronger, smarter, or better in some way; protect them when they're in trouble; or teach them valuable life lessons.

For instance, let's take the example of the Harry Potter series. Both the protagonist (Harry) and the antagonist (Lord Voldemort) of the series are undoubtedly legendary. However, isn't it the outstanding supporting characters like Dumbledore, Ron, and Hermione that give the story an unforgettable touch? That's what a supportive character can do for your story: uplift it in ways you cannot even fathom.

Are you ready to create a supporting character for your story? Here are four criteria that you use to build the foundation of their character. Take a look:

- You must give the supporting character an important role to play in the life of your protagonist.
- Although these characters are integral to the plotline, avoid portraying them as central characters in the scenes of your story.
- The attributes and characteristics of this character should help you create a compelling backdrop for your protagonist.
- The characters that often end up becoming supporting characters are either your protagonist's love interest, their sidekick, underling, mentor, or best friend.

I'm sure you're now starting to understand the depth of the importance of supporting characters in your story.

Let's get started without further ado.

THE IMPORTANCE OF SUPPORTING CHARACTERS FOR YOUR STORY:

In this section, I will do my best to provide you with a detailed account of the importance of supporting characters for your story by telling you how they can help, enhance, and elevate it.

They enrich the character of your protagonist.

As we've discussed earlier, one of the main criteria for a good supporting character is that they should be related or closely associated with your protagonist. This means that through their character, you can tell your readers more about the protagonist than what has been revealed directly in the story. You can enrich your protagonist's past in any number of ways you want using their voice. If your protagonist is alone you can only hear their voice, you don't see the problems from other perspectives. A supporting character is another voice, another point of view, a chance to let your reader hear how decisions are made.

They help nudge the plot forward.

Most writers tend to think that supporting characters only have a small role to play in the story as a whole. However, it might surprise you how much these characters can advance your plot.

These characters add more life to your protagonist's world by acting and reacting to everything that happens to them. In many instances, they might even become the root of conflicts or confusion, which is crucial in pushing the plot forward. As characters, they can fill all those voids that your protagonist cannot and, thus, keep the story moving at a steady pace.

They can help you in creating subplots.

The whole concept of a subplot is that it should revolve around someone other than the protagonist and antagonist. If you have a supporting character, you'll never have to worry about searching for a character. Since the protagonist cannot be expected to handle all story arcs, you can let them worry about the main arc and devote these subplots to your supporting character.

They play a vital role in the development of your story's theme.

As a writer, you must already have thought of the basic themes you want your story to have. But how will you bring up these themes constantly and highlight them to your readers? With a protagonist, it might seem like a difficult job, and that's where your supporting character comes in.

Since these characters are not as central to the plot as the protagonist or antagonist, they will have enough time to highlight your themes for you.

They can heighten the conflict of your plot.

Earlier, we discussed how supporting characters are often at the root of the conflict. But have you wondered how they do it? Through their personality traits or actions. Although these characters are essentially good, they often have some other traits that can eventually lead to conflict. They can be duplicitous, deceptive, or confrontational. These traits might lead to an argument that sets off a chain of events that can lead to a major conflict in the story.

They develop your protagonist's character through interactions.

When you're writing a story, there's only so much you can tell your readers about the protagonist in their own voice. To make the readers really familiar with the protagonists, you'll have to tell them more through the voice of other characters. And what character can do this job better than the supporting character?

Through the interactions between the protagonist and supporting character, you can reveal more about their inner thoughts, feelings, and emotions.

They can be your medium to reveal important information to the readers.

How do you add more suspense to your story? By having interesting information planned for the readers and revealing it slowly and steadily throughout the course of the story. But who will do that job for you? Obviously, you cannot serve this information to them on a silver platter.

It requires proper planning and scheming to keep things interesting in the story, along with a medium that you will use to reveal these secrets. You can count on your supporting characters and burden them with this responsibility.

Are you planning to write a book series? Here's what the supporting characters can do for you.

If you're planning to write multiple books or might be into the idea somewhere down the road, there's more the supporting characters have to offer to you. In your successive books, you can make them the protagonist. In other words, having supporting characters in your story will ensure that you'll always have plenty of material to work with if you ever plan to write a spin-off.

WHAT WILL SUPPORTING CHARACTERS BRING TO THE STORY?

There are three main elements that the supporting characters can add to your story. And these are the contributions that you cannot expect from a protagonist or an antagonist. Not only because they have plenty on their metaphorical plate but also because these elements must come from a neutral place if you want to have the desired effect on your readers.

Let's read about these elements now.

Supporting characters must affect your story in some monumental way.

Once you've drawn a rough sketch of your supporting character, ask yourself this: If I remove this character from the plotline, in what way will it change my story? If your answer is "not so much," it's a clear sign that your supporting character needs more work.

As I said earlier, while you needn't bring these characters into every scene of your story, you must develop them to be important to the central plot. Otherwise, their character wouldn't be strong enough to shoulder all the responsibilities that you expect them to. Simply put, if you want their thoughts, feelings, or ideas to matter to your readers, you must first make them matter to the protagonist and, consequently, the plot of your story.

Supporting characters will influence your protagonist.

Another important question that you must ask yourself while developing this character is: "How does this character impact my protagonist?"

And if you have no clear answer to this question, you must keep working on their character until you can come up with a good one. The main reason why a supporting character is valuable to your story is that they add or provide something valuable (almost priceless) to your protagonist. They could teach them important life lessons, or stand next to them in times of grave troubles, uplift and encourage them when they're at their weakest, and so on. You can take your pick, but make sure they're indispensable to your protagonist. Because, when a character is indispensable to your protagonist, they naturally become indispensable to your readers. They can be used as the main factor that causes the protagonist to drop their lie and accept the truth.

Supporting characters will bring variety and contrast to your story.

Because a supporting character has lesser importance than the protagonist or antagonist, as a writer, you will experience more freedom while building their personality. They could have unique quirks and interests, an extraordinary appearance, and witty expressions. You can give them strange habits or fashion sense to make them stand out from the other major and minor characters, adding more flavor and variety to your story. And when you create such characters, they become etched in the memories of your readers forever.

Now that I've told you everything I believe you need to know about the supporting character, we can proceed to discuss how you will create them for your story.

CREATING SUPPORTING CHARACTERS:

If the idea of creating such a strong supporting character has intimidated you, don't worry, you're not alone. In my early years, I struggled with it as well. But with time, it got easier. Then I devised a ten-step method where I broke down all the key features of the supporting character into ten different pointers to make the task more convenient and effective.

Today, I'm going to share with you these steps that are the secret to my supporting character development:

Step 1: Give Your Supporting Character These Three Features

All great supporting characters must have these three features:

- A character arc: an arc that moves, grows, and evolves alongside the plotline.
- A strong perspective: their perspective will lend them an assertive personality, making your readers take them seriously.
- Clear personality traits: the more definition you add to their personality, the more authentic their character will seem to your readers.

Step 2: Make Their Character Three-Dimensional

Do you remember how we divided all characters of your story into two groups earlier? The first one comprises round characters, which includes both the protagonist and antagonist. The second category is made up of flat characters and includes all characters left behind.

Now, following this rule, many writers tend to create a flat, two-dimensional supporting character. However, the role of your supporting character in your story is more valuable and cannot be fulfilled by a flat character. Therefore, you must add some depth to them—not as much as the protagonist or antagonist, but quite close to it.

Give them hobbies and interests, a family, a job or occupation, a social circle, and a steady backstory. As you figure out these details, you'll learn more about who they are as a person, which will prove to be beneficial later when you place them in difficult circumstances and make note of their thoughts and actions.

Step 3: Make a Rough Chart to Keep Track of Their Development throughout the Plot

Are you familiar with creating and using character charts while writing stories? For those of you who don't use them, you must start right away. It can simplify your job more than you can imagine!

These charts are basically timelines that contain the birthdays, anniversaries, and current age of all major characters. Additionally, the chart also includes all info regarding the ages of your characters in relation to other characters, the years of all-important past and present experiences, and other world events that are central to the plot.

Some writers who use these charts only add the details of the protagonist or antagonist in them, which is a big mistake if you ask me. If you wish to create a three-dimensional supporting character, their timelines and other minor details must be kept track of as well.

Step 4: Make It a Point to Keep Them Interesting

The ground rule for making any character interesting is to stop trying to make them likable or perfect. This is as true for your supporting character as it is for the protagonist and antagonist.

And because your supporting character can have more flexibility than the other leads, you can push more conventional boundaries while creating them. Whatever you plan for their character, make sure it doesn't fit right into their stereotype. Always try to experiment with new things with them.

Step 5: When You Speak through Them, Speak with Purpose

If you look back to all the great stories you've read and loved, you'll find that they all had one character that spoke with purpose. This character had less dialogue than most others, but still, you kept waiting anxiously for them to speak. And they were neither the protagonist nor the antagonist, but a third character we now call a supporting character.

That's the kind of personality you should aim to provide your supporting character with. Whenever you're writing scenes of their interactions with another character, pay special attention to what you want them to say. Every sentence they speak should be filled with purpose, making them one of the most powerful characters in your story.

Step 6: Devote Ample Time to Design the Way They Communicate with Others

Other than filling their voice with power and purpose, there are other things that your supporting character's dialogue can determine. It determines what social class they belong to, how they were brought up, and how they regard others.

Moreover, you can also use their communications and interactions with others to advance your plotline and contribute to your world-building.

Step 7: Provide Them with a Unique, Memorable Name

Most people would wonder, "What's the fuss about a name?" But then, most people aren't great writers. As a promising writer, you must have an eye for details, particularly when you're writing a long story, such as a novel.

Naming your characters is one such minor detail that many writers tend to overlook. But what they forget is that, if you can create or think of something meaningful and extraordinary enough, it will stay with your readers forever, just like the name of your supporting character.

Step 8: Be Ruthless While Creating Them

One thing all readers love in stories is the element of surprise. No matter which genre you pick up, there's always scope for surprise if you do it right.

And because your supporting character is going to be highlighted throughout the story, you can make them as unpredictable as you like, as long as it is within reason or logic. **Step 9: Be Careful about Their Strategic Placement**

Just like the character development of your supporting character is crucial to the plot, how or where you place them in the story is equally important. After you've created their character, sit back and think about when you would introduce them into the story and which major scenes they will be involved in.

Step 10: Don't Try to Create Multiple Supporting Characters

If you've fathomed how intricately you need to create a supporting character you'll realize that, if you do it right, one will be enough. Creating multiple supporting characters in a single story, no matter how long it is, is a marvel only a few have been able to accomplish. If you're writing your first story, I'd strongly recommend against it.

DIFFERENT KINDS OF SUPPORTING CHARACTERS:

If you're a bookworm who has read many stories, you might have noticed that supporting characters are often seen playing one of three roles. These roles can also be divided into three categories, and the supporting character you're creating for your story can be one of them. Let's explore these roles more extensively now:

Supporters:

Just as the name itself suggests, the supporters are the most common type of supporting character you will find in most stories. These characters provide assistance to your protagonist in some way or another.

Taking the example of the Harry Potter series, you can find many supporters here. Be it the Weasley family or Professor McGonagall, all of them supported Harry throughout his journey.

Antagonizers:

The term "antagonizer" is very similar to "antagonist," which itself is suggestive of the antagonizer being a negative character in the story. But what sets them apart from the latter? The fact that they're not the central villain of the plot. In fact, these characters are basically the antithesis of the supporters who try to create minor obstructions in the path of the protagonist.

Draco Malfoy played the part of an antagonizer in the Harry Potter series.

Informers:

The informers are characters that are not closely associated with the protagonist throughout the course of the story. However, they do help them in some major way, often by bringing them meaningful information.

In the Harry Potter series, Sirius Black plays the part of an informer.

CREATING UNFORGETTABLE SUPPORTING CHARACTERS:

Have you already created your supporting character but aren't feeling completely satisfied? Perhaps the character is too bland, or is missing something that you can't quite point out? I might have the solution to your problem.

While everybody wants to learn about the secret to creating unforgettable heroes and villains, it takes true creativity to develop a stellar supporting character. Here are some pointers that can help you add an unforgettable supporting character:

- Read about different typical supporting characters from several stories, identify the stereotype they're following, and then try to ensure that your character is different from those stereotypes.
- If your supporting character is complementary to the protagonist but occasionally opposes the antagonist, the readers have a better chance of liking them.
- Provide your supporting character with at least one defining trait or habit that can set them apart from any character your readers might've read about before.
- The best way to highlight your supporting character is by showing your readers how they impact the lives of your protagonist.
- The backstory of your supporting character is something your readers would definitely want to know more about, so don't keep it from them. Add two elements to these characters: a major flaw and an inner conflict that they have struggled with since the beginning of the story.
- Design a separate character arc for them with a major lesson learned or conflict resolved by the end.

With this, we've reached the end of this chapter. I'm sure you've learned a lot about what supporting characters are and how you can create them for your story. To test your knowledge, I'm going to leave you with a couple of quick exercises.

For the first exercise, you need to think of a story you've read recently and identify its supporting character. Having done that, ask yourself the following questions about this character and see what you can find:

- How does this character help in the advancement of the plot?
- Do they reveal any new information about the protagonist? If they do, have they done it in the best possible way, or was there room for improvement?
- Does the peculiar personality or behavior of this character set the tone for the scenes they're present in?

Now, I have another dinner table exercise that will help you in lending all your characters a unique personality. Don't worry, you won't need a real dinner table for it.

All you need to do is imagine that all the major characters of your story are sitting around a table, having dinner together, and a sudden incident takes place. How would each one of them react to it?

We'll meet again in the next chapter.

CHAPTER 9
DO'S AND DON'TS OF CHARACTER CREATION

So far in the book, we've already covered everything you need to know about all the important elements of your story, including characters, plot, and structure. Within characters, we've discussed the creation of protagonists, antagonists, and supporting characters at length. What now remains are some vital dos and don'ts that you must be careful about while creating these characters.

Keep in mind these are some of the most common mistakes the new or even experienced writers are bound to make in character creation. I hope talking about it here will help you to steer clear of them. Let's get started!

WHAT TO DO IN CHARACTER CREATION:

I'm assuming that you have already created all the major and minor characters of your story. However, as long as your story isn't published yet, there's still room for change and improvement, right?

Here is a basic checklist that you can tick off to ensure that they stand out and make your story extraordinary as a result. Take a look:

Create Characters Who Reflect Your Interests

As a writer, you certainly possess the independence to lend your characters hobbies and interests as varied as possible. You can make them interested in sword-fighting, horse riding, some exclusive martial art, or any such exquisite skill. However, if you're not familiar with these arts or skills yourself, will you really be able to capture their essence? I agree that research can go a long way in bringing your imagination to life, but no matter how ordinary, a real interest is likely to trump a larger-than-life, fictitious one.

Suppose you give your character a basic passion like cooking, gardening, or playing some musical instrument. While it might not sound so exciting, you will certainly be able to give it a personal touch that can attract your readers to you because you feel truly connected to it yourself.

Give Your Characters a Last Name

As budding writers, we often miss some intricate details while creating our characters, and one such mistake is not giving them the last name. Now, you certainly wouldn't forget the last name of your protagonist, their close friends, or the antagonist. However, a story, particularly one as long as a novel, has hundreds of characters, and in the course of writing, it is easy to miss one of their last names.

And what seems like a tiny mistake can take away the air of reality from your story. Is there really any person who doesn't have a last name? Perhaps not. To avoid this mistake, you can prepare a draft where you write out the names of all the characters, no matter how small or insignificant, including their last names. While most of them might not even come up in your story, you will always know their full names on the off chance that they do.

Display the Motives and Emotions of Your Characters through Interactions

Most bookworms crave a story that challenges them and pushes them to think and observe rather than provide them everything on a silver platter. If you aim to write a good story, that's exactly what you need to do. Instead of conveying the thoughts, motives, and ideas of your characters to your readers directly in your or the narrator's voice, you should reveal them through their interactions with each other.

For instance, instead of telling your readers that a character feels insecure or intimidated in the presence of their father, you can make them behave insecurely in their presence and let your readers reach a conclusion on their own.

Give Your Characters Interiority

Unless all your characters narrate their own story within your novel, your readers will know almost everything about them through their communications and interactions with other characters. But have you noticed how, in real life, the assumptions or perceptions that others have of you can be different from who you really are? That's what interiority is all about.

To give your characters interiority, you must provide the readers with a comparison between how the characters see themselves and how other characters see them. For example, not everyone you know would describe you in the same way; they have all had different interactions with you and see different things. This variation in a story makes the character seem real.

Describe the Physical World around Your Characters in Detail

Every good story provides its readers an intimate view of their characters' world: their surroundings, neighborhood, school, college, or workspace. It helps the reader put themselves in the shoes of these characters and live vicariously through them. This is exactly what you need to do for your story.

If you're not successful in intricately building your character's world and miss out on even some minor details, your readers will never be able to form a clear picture of it inside their heads and will struggle to connect with them. And trust me, that's not a risk you should be willing to take.

Skip the Detailed Physical Characteristics of All Characters

I know that at first glance, this point seems to be contradicting the last one, but it really isn't. Describing the world of your characters is very different from describing the characters themselves.

While it is paramount to describe the physical attributes of your central characters in detail, you needn't do so for all the other characters. When it comes to the minor characters, you should only provide the readers enough details for them to form a rough sketch in their heads. If you describe these characters too extensively, it will only end up slowing your plot's pace and adding fluff that nobody will remember later anyway. I like to use the look-a-like trick, it's short and it easily sticks in people's minds. For example if you said the character's name was William Faps and he was thin with a large nose and kind of looked like Wile E. Coyote, then that's all you need sometimes. Your readers will remember that perfectly.

Provide Your Characters with the Right Skills

When you're deciding the skills, hobbies, and interests of your minor characters, make sure that they have a role to play in your central plot. If you can do this successfully, you'll observe how they help advance your plot rather than obstruct it.

Surprise Your Readers by Contradicting Their Expectations

As I've already discussed, all readers enjoy an element of surprise in the stories they read. As a writer, you can use this knowledge to your benefit while creating your characters.

Once your readers have grown familiar with the characters of your story and have started to predict their actions and reactions, give them a surprise! Make your characters react in a way they'd never have expected. However, it is also important to do this within the reason or logic of your story. **Learn How to Use Stereotypes to Your Benefit**

No matter what people might say about stereotypes, at the end of the day, these stereotypes bring them comfort because of their familiarity. You can also incorporate stereotypes into your story and then flip them upside down midway and shock your readers.

For instance, create a young, innocent boy whom everybody loves and even takes advantage of. Then, when your readers have already developed feelings of sympathy for him, show them how he is secretly obsessed with hurting animals or a shoplifter or something else that contradicts the personality you've created for him so far.

Develop an Intimate Relationship with Your Characters

Before you begin to write your story, make sure you know all your characters intimately. Now you might be wondering how this could help your story? It's not related to your story directly. However, it might improve your efficiency in writing the story.

When you're familiar with your characters, you will not have to spend as much time thinking about their actions and reactions to the events within your story.

Be Bold Enough to Take Risks

No writer has ever created an extraordinary character while remaining within their comfort zone. This is something you must keep in mind when you are creating your characters. Give them something new, something that you haven't read or seen in another story so far. While this might seem like a gamble at the moment, it could ultimately make your whole story unique.

Add Variety to Your Characters

As you already know, your readers all have different personalities, beliefs, and thought processes. This means that not all of them might necessarily connect with your protagonist or antagonist.

Therefore, if you want a majority of your readers to be able to connect to your characters, make sure that you create them diversely, giving them different personalities, interests, thoughts, and beliefs.

WHAT NOT TO DO IN CHARACTER CREATION:

Once you've checked off all the points we discussed in the last section, here are some things that you should absolutely not do while creating the characters. If you've already done any of these, it's time for you to revisit those characters and make some edits.

Don't Create Characters That Are Too Perfect

As we've discussed throughout the book, no character who is perfect has ever gained a place in the heart of a reader. In fact, most readers don't gel with such characters because they set unrealistic expectations for them and for people in general.

Therefore, if you want to create a character that your readers can connect to, ditch the pursuit of perfection and get real.

Nobody is perfect so why should your character be perfect?

Don't Base Your Characters Completely Off of Real People

It is understood that, as writers, we often base our characters on real-life people; it could be someone we know intimately or someone we're only acquainted with. However, drawing inspiration is one thing—basing your characters around them entirely is another. There's a very thin line between the two, and if you cross it, the reality of the person you've drawn said character from might start influencing them in more ways than you initially planned for, pushing you into a creative block.

Don't Focus Too Hard on a Single Flaw

As writers, when we're creating a minor character we make a rough outline of their personality beforehand. In most cases, we lend them some important attribute or flaw first and then fill in the gaps to make a well-rounded character. In this process, it is a common mistake to base their whole character around that one flaw or tendency.

Always remember that these characters will be real people within your story, and no real person can be defined by a single skill or quality. They're bound to have their own likes, dislikes, and individual ideas.

Don't Make Your Characters' Lives Too Easy or Uncomplicated

All of you will agree that no person has changed for the better from within their comfort zone. In order to grow, they need to feel some discomfort. The same is true for the characters of your story. If all of them have a decent life—a loving family, steady income, fulfilled dreams, and ambitions —why would your readers want to read about them? This is more or less similar to creating a perfect character, as we've discussed earlier.

Instead of doing this, you should put struggles and challenges into their lives that push their boundaries and force them to change and grow into a stronger and smarter version of themselves.

Don't Be Obsessed with Stereotypes

While it is easier for readers to connect to stereotypes because of the familiarity they've developed, it doesn't mean adding too many stereotypical characters in your story will lend it a higher appeal.

Always remember that your characters should be in sync with your story, not your readers. If you can create characters that complement your story by fitting right into the plot, your readers have a higher chance of liking it.

Don't Dump Information about Your Characters All at Once

It is no secret that all readers prefer characters that have multiple layers peeled off steadily throughout the story over those whom they know everything about from day one. The latter will often appear as a static, even stagnant character which can easily seem unrealistic to your readers.

Your readers enjoy new, interesting things throughout the course of the story, which keeps them hooked until the very end. And if these interesting things are coming from your characters, it is even better. Moreover, info-dumping can also seem a little overwhelming to your readers and might lead them to quit reading midway. Therefore, you should ease them into your story slowly and steadily. When working out your storyline it's a good thing to decide when to offer certain bits of information to the reader.

Don't Be Afraid to Cut Out Information

Toward the end of the story, some writers might start feeling that it has stretched out longer than necessary. If you're one of those, you needn't worry at all; this happens to the best of us.

However, as a new writer, you might feel more attached to your work and, thus, more hesitant to cut out any part you've written, even if it isn't directly relevant to the story. But trust me, a story that stretches long is not going to do any good to you or your readers. If you don't want your readers to quit reading because it's too long, act while you still have time and opportunity. As they say, the pain of an injection is better than that of the disease. They call it "kill your darlings" and it can be difficult to lose something you've spent so much time over.

Don't Be Afraid to Change Your Viewpoint Character if Needed

Planning the outline of your plot and character arcs before you start writing your story is certainly helpful. However, if you expect all your characters to pan out exactly as you planned beforehand, you are in for some serious surprises.

The truth, when you bring your outlined characters to life while writing the story, they're naturally exposed to the possibility of change. At some points, a supporting character or any other minor character might even seem to be stealing the thunder from your protagonist. However, this needn't send you into a panic. It is quite natural to happen and will not impact your story negatively. The best thing you can do is set the initial pace and let the characters follow their course.

Don't Disclose All Details of Your Characters Just Because You Know Them

The most important thing that you need to learn about story writing is how to separate yourself from your characters and view and portray them objectively. This is a lesson most writers learn with time. Initially, as a new writer, you might feel deeply connected to your characters and live through them. However, this shouldn't interfere with your story. A good story is one that has suspense among its characters so that the readers can feel it more acutely. If you get carried away and disclose everything before the right time, it might spoil the suspense in the story.

With this, we come to the end of this chapter. I hope all the dos and don'ts I've talked about have helped you in giving a better shape to your characters and, thereby, elevated your story. In the next chapter, I'll tell you how you can take your story to the next level.

CHAPTER 10

TAKING YOUR STORY TO THE NEXT LEVEL

Have you already finished writing your story? It must be an exciting time for you, feeling victorious and nervous all at once. What's the next step in your plan? Editing, proofreading, and then forwarding the draft to a publishing house? Well, before you reach the last step, here are some simple tricks that you can incorporate into your story while editing it to elevate its level. Most of these pointers might already be within your story, so you needn't worry. Let's proceed.

HOW TO TAKE YOUR STORY TO THE NEXT LEVEL:

Whenever it's time for me to edit and proofread my story, I always keep a list of ten pointers handy to check off to make sure my story will be as appealing to my readers as it is to me. Here are the ten pointers that do the trick for me. I hope they can elevate your story efficiently as well:

Show, Don't Tell

As a writer, you are obviously reciting your story to the readers. However, the readers don't want it narrated, do they?

For a story to catch your readers' attention thoroughly, they have to live the story; envision it, and not only listen to it in your voice. It is for this very reason that most writers prefer to make a character their narrators instead of saying it themselves; for example, you don't need to say the character felt jealous when you can show the jealousy through their actions. Perhaps they squeeze a flower so tightly it is crushed.

All you need to make sure of is that you're always describing an incident as it is really happening rather than explaining it. This should be done for all major events and occurrences in your story.

Go Beyond the Primary Senses: Body Language

Almost all writers need to have a good grasp of capturing the senses of vision and sound in their story by describing the way people, cities, and things look and sound. But if you've ever read a great story, you must have noticed how they seem better the more you can visualize the events.

That's exactly what you need for your story to succeed among your editors and readers. Of the other things that can elevate your story, the body language of your characters is an important one. You know that a person's body language can say a lot about what they're thinking or feeling; your characters are no exception to this. You can convey a lot through how they act and react to every major or minor event without even using many words. Doing this will add more depth and texture to your story. Let's use an example of a line without body language. "John stopped and lit a cigarette; he exhaled a stream of smoke at the windowpane."

Now, let's try it with body language: "John stopped and lit a cigarette. He rested it close to his chest and his eyes stared dreamily through the window. He exhaled slowly through the rising curls of smoke."

Body language is a universal language and can explain more than just words.

Embrace the Idiosyncrasies

Are you one of those writers who try to make their characters logical or reasonable all the time? Well, you might be able to pull off such characters in your story, but keep in mind that hardly anyone can be reasonable and sane-minded all the time in real life, especially if unusual things are happening as they often do in stories. And since your goal should be to make your characters as lifelike as possible, giving them an outburst or two will not harm your story but elevate it. A character's strangeness will keep your readers guessing throughout the story; it will keep them glued, as they try to piece together theories.

If your readers can predict everything your characters do or say, they'll feel bored in no time, wanting to read another, more interesting story. But if they can sense the unpredictability of these characters, they will feel compelled to keep reading. Don't worry, not all your characters need to be unpredictable; one or two might be enough.

Make some of your characters act strangely or unexpectedly due to love, anger, or sorrow—emotions that often get the best of us in real life.

I recommend taking your weakest character and brainstorming some unusual characteristics for them; perhaps they like to steal items from people's houses or they just can't be polite to pretty girls.

Take a character and make them obsessed with something; it does happen to people and it can make them do some crazy things. Jealousy is another reason people go crazy and lose their composure. Experiment with it and remember to make it interesting.

Forget about Being Pretty

Most writers have a tendency to make their stories about everything pretty and decorative; they don't delve into the darker side of life or the world for the sake of staying in control and avoiding conflicting reactions from their readers. But let me tell you one thing: All of us have a darker side that we shouldn't keep hidden forever. And if your story is all about happy and pretty things, what will it give your readers to think about after they put the book down?

I can assure you that all of us have read or heard countless such stories and have forgotten all about them. And it's not even your fault that they slipped from your mind. There is nothing remarkable about stories like that. And, if you don't want your story to be forgotten in the crowd, be prepared to get your hands dirty.

You must be courageous enough to show feelings of fear, shamelessness, and contempt in your story. There are subjects that aren't attractive like racism or incest and it is normal to want to avoid these subjects for fear of upsetting the readers but if it's really what you wanted to write about then you should. It will not only elevate your writing but also free it from all kinds of mental shackles. And when that happens, you'll unleash your true potential as a writer.

Be True to Your IQ

Most writers make an effort to dumb down their stories in order to attract a larger population of readers. But if I'm honest, those who truly enjoy reading books are both welleducated to appreciate your writing and wealthy enough to buy your books.

Moreover, dumbing down your story for your readers has another major disadvantage. In the process of doing so, you might lose the true essence of your writing without even knowing it. To keep that from happening, you must not underestimate your readers and resist trying to overexplain everything to them.

Use Your Best Material Only When It Serves a Purpose

Have you ever heard the phrase "saving the best for the last"? Well, if you want to elevate the level of your story, that's certainly one of the most efficient ways to go about it. When you're creating an outline for your story, you must have noted several interesting elements to add to the story in order to liven it up. And while writing, there might be several instances where you'll feel tempted to use one just because the story appears to be dragging along. But if you truly want to create a good story, don't give in to the temptation. Trust your planning and let these interesting events unfold in their own time.

Some writers also go out of their way to make their story interesting by adding unusual interactions or events.

However, before you do that, ask yourself, "Is this relevant to the plotline even remotely?" Because if they are not directly relevant to the story, your readers will ultimately end up questioning their very existence in the story. And if you cannot provide them with an answer, it will take them mere minutes to decide that your story wasn't worth their time.

Make Your Readers Laugh

As a writer, you must know that, as a general rule, your editor and reader might look for different things in your story. And a good story is the one that satisfies them both equally. But do you know what that one thing that both these people are looking for is? It's wit.

No matter what genre your readers are looking for, at the end of the day, all they want is to be entertained; to laugh and forget the mundanity or worries of their everyday lives, even if just for a moment. And as writers, it is our job to provide them with it.

To be honest, making your readers laugh isn't as difficult as it might sound to some. It doesn't require a particularly high IQ to conjure up scenarios that are bound to be funny. Here are some quick, subtle tactics that you can employ to make your readers laugh while reading your story:

- Present them with absurd imagery that they might not be expecting.
- Add a witty banter between two of the characters that your readers might enjoy.
- Look for opportunities where you can find small incongruities in your characters where you can incorporate witty scenes and interactions.

We laugh at absurdities others can't see, we laugh when we are surprised, and we laugh when we are caught off guard.

Perhaps your character has a blind spot that causes amusement. Try and capitalize on your character's wit rather than your plot.

Make Your Readers Cry

Have you ever read a story where you've laughed and cried? If you have, I'm sure you will remember the name of both the story and its writer forever. And while making people laugh is not that difficult, it takes real skill to make them cry. Wondering why? It is because people will only cry over something when they're deeply attached to it. And if you can make the readers connect to your story or its characters on that level, you've already succeeded in creating a good story.

Now, let's get down to discussing how you can make this happen for your story. As I've just mentioned, the readers need to feel overcome with emotions in order to cry. Here are some tricks that can help you achieve this:

- Plan your pathos from the very beginning of the story.
- Plant the seed of emotions quite early in the story because it will take the readers some time to build their intensity.
- Make your readers familiar with the vulnerability of your characters.
- Add some typical characters that readers can easily feel compassion for, such as young children, a woman who has to take care of her family, a man who is struggling to succeed in life, and so on.

On a personal level, I seem to be a sucker for an uplifting speech; when the underdogs are facing annihilation and the hero steps in to motivate his followers, these make me emotional. Also, unselfish acts seem to get my tears flowing. To be honest any strong emotional connection between two characters has the potential to make readers well up. Use what works on you and it should work for others.

Keep Some Information Hidden from Your Readers

How many of you are aware of Ernest Hemingway's iceberg theory of writing? It is a strategy that's quite popular in fiction writing and states that if the information about the characters and events of your story is an iceberg, a large portion of it should remain underwater, with your readers being able to see only its tip.

But when did he plan to reveal the whole iceberg to his readers? Never. This is where things get interesting. Hemingway believed that spoon-feeding everything to the readers wasn't how stories should be written. He proposed that the readers should comprehend the underlying themes and meanings on their own.

When you write your story using this theory, you will leave a lot of room for your readers' imaginations to wander. And every reader loves a book that compels them to think.

Go with the Active Voice as Much as Possible

All of us know that the noun-verb-object structure of sentences is the most uncomplicated one. But what you might not know is that it is also the most engaging one. While experimenting with other aspects of your story is healthy, you should try to stick to an active voice as far as possible when it comes to the language. It is because your readers can read active voice more easily and will, thus, be captivated by the story until the very end.

PRACTICES THAT CAN HELP TO DEVELOP YOUR WRITING:

Now that your story's finished and has probably been sent to your editor, what is your next move? While some of you might want to go back to your daily life and pursue your old profession, there might be some who want to continue to write.

If you're still reading, I'm assuming you're a member of the latter group. And in that case, I have some tricks and tips that I practice in between my large writing projects so that I can continue to grow as a writer. If you want to do the same, check these tips out:

Try Your Hand at All Kinds of Writing

While writing novels is quite popular, you must acknowledge the fact that there's more to creative writing than just novels. And as a writer, your growth lies in broadening your scope. I can understand the initial hesitation to try out other styles, but if you don't push yourself to get over it, it's an indication that you've found your comfort zone and refuse to step out of it. And, as you already know, no great achievements have ever come from one's comfort zone.

If you're a novelist, in between writing novels you should also try your hands at writing short stories and explore both fiction and non-fiction writing. For more variety, you can even start a blog and see how it turns out. After all, you might never know the diversity of your writing skills unless you put it to the test.

Make It a Point to Write Every Day

All the writers who have left their mark in literature made it a point to make writing a priority, not a hobby that they came back to when they had free time. For instance, Stephen King disclosed in an interview that he assigns himself 2,000 words to write on a daily basis.

When you write every day, you can't expect everything you write to be a masterpiece. But, rest assured that every single piece you write, be it a story, a blog, an article, or a poem, is going to contribute something to your writing skills.

To make your commitment toward writing easier on you, you can join a writer's community or set your daily writing hours and plan your schedule around it.

Set Milestones to Keep Yourself Going

When you're writing a novel, does the high word count or number of pages make you feel nervous or overwhelmed? Trust me when I say that you're not the first writer to feel that way. As a general rule, most novels are generally between 70,000 and 85,000 words long—that kind of volume can intimidate any writer, particularly those who are doing it for the first time.

If you want to overcome this intimidating feeling and remain moti-vated, milestones are the way to go. Break your novel into several smaller parts (or chapters) and assign yourself small goals that you can achieve on a daily or weekly basis. If you keep going in this manner, you'll finish your novel before you even realize it.

Don't Ignore the Importance of Breaks

A common mistake that most writers make is trying to avoid taking breaks while writing. For instance, suppose you have come up with a great writing idea? Would you sit down immediately and keep writing until you're exhausted without taking any break? Well, that's not the right way and can affect your creativity and general efficiency.

Instead, what you can do is record a voice note of your idea then and there, and then complete what you were doing and make a plan on when and how to write your story.

Even while you are writing your story, there will be days when you will feel blue and don't want to touch your keyboard at all. In the writer's community, we call it writer's block, which is something all writers are subject to. So, instead of pushing yourself on these days, you should give yourself a break and do what makes you happy, even if it means taking a long nap or playing with your dog all day. I promise you that the next morning, you're going to wake up feeling refreshed and motivated, ready to get back to writing.

Read More to Write More

Do you think that it's a mere coincidence that all great writers also happen to be avid readers? Because it is not. What or how much you read can play a major role in shaping up your personality as a writer. Because it is often through reading that most of us find our creative muse or individual voice.

Actively Seek Feedback and Incorporate It into Your Writing

Even if you're one of the most professional writers, it is impossible to detach yourself completely from your writing and critique it unbiasedly. This is why it helps to have writer friends who can read your fiction pieces and critique them fairly. While you might feel insecure about it in the beginning, keep in mind that an outsider's opinion on your writing, particularly those who are writers themselves, can help you learn your most valuable lessons.

SECRETS THAT CAN HELP YOU WRITE FASTER:

As someone who has been acquainted with creative writing for a long time, I've learned that writing is not something that you can rush. It's a process that can best proceed without any external pressure or stress. With that being said, not all of us can afford the luxury of time.

If you're someone who's running behind schedule and are stressed about the deadline, these tips can help you write faster:

Write on a Computer That Has No Internet Connection

All of us are well aware of the fact that the internet can be your worst enemy while writing. It is such a broad, diverse platform offering tones of temptations that can distract you from the task at hand—in this case, writing.

If you are truly devoted to writing or have no time to waste, the first thing you need to do is get rid of your internet connection while writing.

Carry a Notebook Everywhere to Jot Down Your Ideas

All writers will agree with me when I say that writers are never off-duty. You can have a creative idea in the middle of the night or while hanging out with friends or on vacation. If you don't want to lose these rare pearls of wisdom, carry a notebook with you that is dedicated solely to writing down all of your creative ideas and prompts. Trust me; you'll be glad for doing it.

Create an Outline First

An outline is like a blueprint of your story, which you can always refer to when you feel stuck midway. When you're in a rush to finish your story, you'll notice how having an outline can fast-track the process considerably.

Write Now, Edit Later

Most writers have a tendency to keep re-reading their work and editing it every chance they get. You might not notice it, but this constant editing can take up a lot of your time and offer you little in return because you'll still have to edit the whole story after finishing it anyway. So, why bother doing it in between?

Do Your Research after Writing

While doing research and writing hand-in-hand might work well for shorter writing pieces, when you're writing a novel, researching simultaneously will only slow you down. To avoid it from happening, you should keep a paper or file handy wherein you can note down all the research points you can think of while writing and then look them up once you're done for the day.

Two Letters That Will Speed Up Your Writing

The letters are "TK" and strangely enough they mean "to come." At any time that you come to something in your story that needs researching or some serious thought to get the section just right, leave a TK and come back to it later, the TKs can be sorted during the final edit. Why fill in all the details now if it's later going to be cut from the story? It keeps the work flowing and prevents you from stopping. For example, write "evilshopkeepersnameTK" or "spookyfactorydescriptionTK." It's purposely been written as one word in order not to confuse it with the final copy. You can TK full chapters if needed, just to keep the flow going.

Use the Talk-to-Text Feature

Did you know that Google Docs has a feature that allows you to speak your words onto the page instead of typing them? It can be a real lifesaver for the writer who is in a rush or on a strict deadline that's dreadfully close.

Practice Writing Sprints

As you already know, sprinting is basically running as fast as you can within a limited amount of time. But how do you incorporate it into your writing? By setting a timer for ten minutes and trying to squeeze in as much writing as possible within the timeframe. As you become acquainted with this practice, you can increase your time slowly and write faster.

With this, we've reached the ultimate end. I've shared with you all the insights, lessons, tricks, and tips about writing stories that I've gathered over the years. I hope my accumulated knowledge can help you in writing your story.

CONCLUSION

Writing stories is an art, and while mastering this art might involve a lot of work, it is not an unachievable feat. If you're a writer who is writing your first story, the whole task might seem quite intimidating to you. But you mustn't let it get the best of you; to write a great story, all you need to focus on is keeping the reader hooked. And if you proceed with only this goal in mind, you have the potential to become one of the greatest writers of your time.

All stories are supported by eight pillars, namely, plot, structure, characters, point of view, setting, narrative, style, and theme. Out of these elements, the first three are the most crucial to your story and are also referred to as the holy trinity. The plot is the basic sequence of events and happenings that are strung together to make one whole story. The second pillar is the structure of your story, which can help you in choosing the right sequence for your story and keep the outline organized and easy to follow.

The third and most important element of your story is its characters. It is no secret that all stories, no matter how extraordinary their plotline or structure might be, are only successful when they have characters that your readers can connect with. After all, it is these characters that add life to your otherwise factitive story. Some writers believe that a story can have only one major character that all readers focus on: the protagonist. Yet other writers state that in order to write a successful story, both its protagonist and antagonist should be well-rounded characters. But only those who have truly mastered the art of storytelling would agree that your entire story cannot solely depend on a hero or villain, or even a combination of both.

When you're planning to write a story, the first step is generally to create outlines of all your characters, along with their arcs. And, while creating characters might not seem that difficult, creating characters who are unforgettable to your readers is a different thing altogether. There are many ways to add appeal to your characters' personalities. Some of the basic tricks are to lend them a major flaw, a vulnerability that gives them a humane touch, making them seem more lifelike to your readers. You can also add more depth to their arcs by adding more obstructions on their path, raising the stakes of the climax continually, and highlighting their virtues.

In the end, there might be numerous new ways of writing a story, but the elements that add magic to your words and lure in the readers still remain the same, classic ones. As a writer, you must stay true to yourself; draw from real-life experiences; avoid running behind perfection; create real, living, and breathing characters that your readers can identify with; and add some witty bits every now and then to break the monotony. Another indispensable suggestion for writing good stories is not to underestimate the holy trinity; devote plenty of time and effort toward building the plot, designing the structure, and creating compelling characters that will be etched in your readers' minds forever.

Now that I've equipped you with all the weapons that have helped me carve out my journey of creative writing, what are you waiting for? Now is as good a time as any to take a pen and notebook (or a laptop or typewriter, if you prefer) and get to it. I can understand that beginning can be daunting for most new writers. But trust me when I say this: no one is going to help you if you haven't got your own back. Don't let all the rules, techniques, and methods we talked about intimidate you or weigh down. Just start writing your first words and let

your thoughts flow; you'll easily incorporate all the tools and tech-
niques on the way.

If my book has helped you in any way in the course of your writing
journey, I'd love to hear more about it. After all, there's nothing more
satisfying than being able to help others write their stories and achieve
their dreams.

If you enjoyed this book please leave me some feedback by following
this link: My Book https://f2edg3.systeme.io/johnswarner

PART TWO
BOOK 2

THE SECRETS TO
CREATING CHARACTER ARCS
WORKBOOK

An all-inclusive working guide for creating outstanding characters and riveting conflict for writers

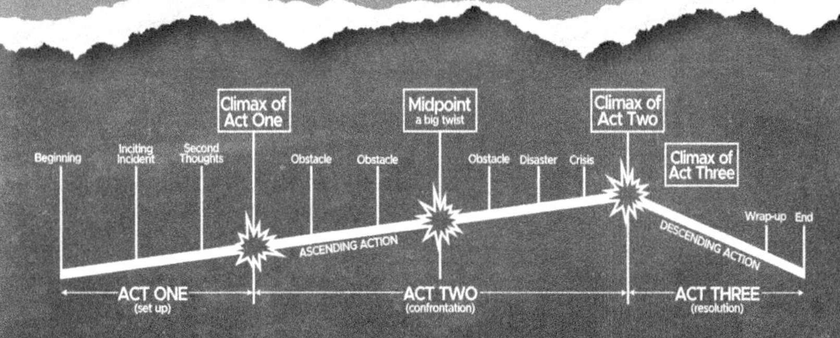

JOHN S WARNER

INTRODUCTION

When we attach ourselves to characters, we steal a part of their reflection and keep it with us forever. That's the kind of magic a writer does when working on the Character Arcs.

Reading habits develop from our formative years, and if you have to name a few children's books off the top of your head, you'll realize most of them have a character's name or reference in the title – *Alice's Adventures in the Wonderland, The Wizard of Oz, Charlie and the Chocolate Factory, Winnie the Pooh, The Lion, the Witch, and the Wardrobe, The tale of Peter Rabbit,* and the list is inexhaustible! Why do you think a character's name features in so many of the classics we grew up reading? The reason is simple–people may forget every nitty-gritty or artistic details that went into creating an extraordinary fiction, but they would certainly remember a memorable character. As a child, I would not have cared if Charlie found his golden ticket and got a chance to see Willie Wonka's chocolate factory from the inside unless I liked the boy and could relate to him in the first place. That also includes Grandpa Joe, who is the merry tritagonist in the story. That's why creating relatable, unforgettable, and remarkable characters is crucial to the craft of fiction writing. Hence, learning how to write compelling character arcs is one of the most essential skills for any writer to keep readers stay invested in your character's destiny, to cheer for them, laugh and cry with them, and critique and empathize with them all along!

Every great story has emotions, actions, ulterior motives, conflicting interests, a higher purpose or a greater good, and a greater than the story-level subtext to it. But the most crucial element is how all of this is expressed. Your characters are the light of the story, the human intervention, and the modus operandi of your more significant artistic goals, which take your story to your readers. Thus, it is vital to focus on their development throughout the book.

Let's say you have a favorite character in the Marvel series, say the Black Panther, for instance. Have you ever thought about what attracts you to this character? Maybe because of:

- His superhuman strength, speed, and power to draw upon strength and knowledge.
- His reflexes, intelligence, endurance, agility, senses, and stamina.
- His martial art skills and action hero personality.
- His curiosity towards inventions or because he is a highly proficient tactician and a great human by heart.

These are some characteristics that the writer developed for Black Panther to make him relatable or convincing. So, this is how you think when developing your characters, and this book will help you devise your character arcs by taking you one step ahead of just the theory of it. The workbook section gives you a hands-on practical experience to hone your skills in a character arc formation. So let's begin!

The foundations of storytelling are not just about what happens in your story but also how it affects each character's journey along the way. There are two main types of characters, and I am not categorizing them moral choice-wise but development-wise: flat and round characters. A flat character is one who stays the same from the beginning through the middle to the end. For example, the Joker in The Dark

Knight is a flat character; though a dynamic and assertive representation, he remains a symbol of motiveless malignity from beginning to end, like Shakespeare's Iago in *Othello*. However, in the same movie, if you look at Harvey Dent, you'll clearly understand what a round character is. A character who shows a positive growth or, as in Harvey's case, a deterioration, a metamorphosis from the beginning to the end, is a round character. Based on these categories of round and flat characters, there are three primary character arcs that you need to master: the positive change arc, the flat arc, and the negative change arc.

Quick question:

Would you like to see a round character or a flat one, and why?

____

____

____

____

____

If your answer is a round character, you must be a fan of transformative character arcs. The changes that take place in a character throughout their arc are what make them so fascinating. It can be emotional, physical, intellectual, spiritual, or mental. Change is the highlight, whether they're changing themselves or other people around them. Stories always focus on how individuals grow and change over time to become better human beings. The writer must probe into the psychological processes to emphasize the arcs of change in character delineation. For example, people love to see a character evolve and rise from dire circumstances to prosperous situations in life. Remember Simba from The Lion King? What strings did the writer pull to make Simba relatable to the audience? Simba's vulnerability as a cub, his guilt because of a good heart, the odds against him being heavier than his tiny shoulders, and his genuine goodness rewarded by a stroke of destiny earn the audience's empathy. But what really wins the audience is his transformation, his rising to the occasion and taking his rightful ways in the order of things, his winning over the ghosts of the past and vanquishing the evil uncle Scar to become 'the Lion King.' People wanted him to rise from the bad times to the good times and cheer for him because he is instrumental in bringing those good times for himself and his pride of lions. So, what character arc do you think that was? A round or flat arc? A positive or negative one? Simba's was a powerful yet relatable positive character arc that connected with the audience because not just the audience connects with his emotional journey; they want good things for him, and when he achieves that, it leaves a smile on the audience's faces.

Can you define a character with whom you relate the most and why?

- Define its characteristics

- Define what's the most empowering part of the character

- What he/she lacks

- What is his strength

Character Arcs Are Necessary to Transform Stories - And Here's Why!

You must have heard about the archetypal debate of the relative importance of plot and character. Aristotle, in his *Poetics*, gave the plot a superior place over character, as it is the action that speaks to the audience / reader, and the action is contained in the plot. However, I believe this leads to pretty lopsided reading because it leaves characters without agency. Hence, in Greek tragedies, destiny plays a more significant role than character. But as you come to Shakespearean tragedies, you'll realize the character is destiny. That is, the protagonist has the agency to make, or unmake, their destiny.

Character and plot cannot exist without each other! If the plot is action, action is executed by the character. Hence, they are symbiotic; both operate synchronically throughout any given story or script. Story-telling is the third product of this synchronization of character and plot, the character's transformation / evolution throughout the different plot points and the transformation, in its turn, shaping the plot development.

This book will look at the five types of character arcs found in storytelling. Remember the three major character arcs: positive change, flat and negative change. These can further be categorized into two positive ones—the positive change arc and flat arc, and three negative arcs—the disillusionment arc, the fall arc, and the corruption arc.

How to Use This Workbook

In this workbook, you will find out how to create engaging character arcs by following the principles of character development. You will also get step-by-step guidance for crafting each essential structural element that goes into character portrayal and practice the theories by responding to specific questions. In the subsequent chapters for each character arc, you will get acquainted with the different stoppages in your character's journey—the lies they believe in, the ghosts they are haunted by, their wants and needs, what they think they want and what they actually want to the point of becoming what they ought to become in the end. You will also get an evolutionary itinerary of the character through different plot points. As you read and analyze the content, you can also try out what you learned in the practice spaces by answering the given questions. The practice spaces in the book are your canvas where you can practice writing and drawing illustrations so that you get to keep running notes on your reading. By the time you finish the workbook, you will have your own template or at least a rough sketch of your fictional character gallery.

Choose the Character Arc You Will Use In This Workbook

Choosing which character arc suits your story's character development best is an important decision. Sometimes you may have a story in an inspired moment, and as you go along, the characters pop in and develop with the plot. If you are a pantser, you definitely find this technique handy. But this has a downside—you might lose sight of where your characters are headed; they can go haywire and may not align with the desired effects of the story. Hence giving character development a lot of forethought before diving into writing is the way to go, and that's where this character arcs workbook can serve you best. By trying out different arcs, you get the hang of what works best to your story's demands. A clear view of the characters gives your plot a proper direction and makes the writing process several notches more manageable and less chaotic.

Imagine now there is a story in your mind and answer these questions in the flow of it:

Q1. How does your story start?

____

____

____

____

____

Q2. What are the types of characters you think of?

____

____

____

____

____

____

Q3. What are the arcs behind the characters that decide the best story?

____

____

____

____

____

____

Q4. Why do you pick a specific arc for a particular character?

CHAPTER 1
WHAT'S IN A POSITIVE CHANGE ARC?

Ask yourself an honest question as a reader—would you care to see a person deteriorate or rise up to the occasion in course of a fictional journey? Most of the time, characters shape their own destiny, good or bad, but as readers engaging with them we expect to get inspired by fiction and that can only happen if the character undergoes what we call a 'hero's journey', like Simba from *The Lion King*, for instance.

Hence, the positive change arc is one of the most popular arcs in storytelling. Also called a Hero's Journey, it is a positive transformational arc that often results in an objectively happy ending. Regardless of the protagonist's external circumstances, they will be a better version of themselves and better off circumstantially by the end. The more serious their psychological and emotional struggles, or the higher the stakes or the odds the greater is the transformation. These struggles and predicaments that chisel the character into a better version or transform them completely into a refined self are both internal and external. The Character starts with the belief that something is holding them back from being whole and empowered—these can be some self-delusional lies the character believes in, an incorrect estimation of their own worth or some baggage from the past. But as soon as they plunge into the conflict covered in the plot, they are forced into personal growth, which eventually allows them to reject their old ways of thinking in favour of new ones.

For example, Scrooge is an unpleasant protagonist in Charles Dickens' *A Christmas Carol*. He is selfish, greedy, and insensitive at the beginning of the story, but through his trials with the three Christmas ghosts that haunt him, he finds out what makes life worth living: compassion! The ghosts obviously aren't real, but a metaphor for the voice of his own conscience, his introspection and self-evaluation leading to a refined perspective. Ultimately, he succeeds in differentiating what's worth chasing in life and what's not; he is free from the shackles of his old self and that is a true hero's journey!

YOUR CHARACTER AND ITS LIE

Let's start with the assumption that a character lacks something in life. The missing piece can be anything: a profession, a relationship, or a purpose in life. They are not lacking something external to them but rather an essential part of themselves that they discover in course of their journey.

Let's revisit the Lion King's example. Why does Simba run away? He is made to believe by his crafty uncle Scar that he is responsible for his father's death, that had he not needed protection from the herd, his father wouldn't have met his awful end. So he keeps blaming himself and runs away from home, Hoping never to return. This lie, he believes, leaves him feeling incomplete on the inside, and he finds the broken piece, what's missing inside through fighting his uncle and, most importantly, fighting his guilt. He realized that he could only honor his father's sacrifice by becoming the rightful king of the jungle and doing his unfinished work. Defeating Scar is an external outcome of overcoming his deeply held misconception about himself and embracing his destiny. It's a journey from self-delusional lies to truth, more internal than external.

Exercise #1: Write down six possible variations of the lie your character believes. Specify and describe them.

____

____

____

____

____

____

THE CHARACTER'S SYMPTOMS OF LIE

When looking for the symptoms of a lie in your Character's life, consider what they do and how they react to different situations. The signs of his lie are evident in their actions, though the character may not be completely aware of those symptoms.

Exercise #1: Answer the following questions now.

Question #1: Select the following symptoms in your Character's life.

- Hurt

____

____

____

- Revenge

____

____

____

- Fear

____

____

____

- Guilt

____

____

____

- Shame

____

____

____

- Past regrets

____

____

____

WHAT'S THE THING YOUR CHARACTER NEEDS

Unmet needs can significantly impact your character's growth. In some stories, this will only cause minor changes to how they interact with other people and situations. Still, in every case, there is usually an internal transformation, where they view themselves and what remains of their external life. These needs, sometimes known and sometimes unknown to the character, necessitate and catalyze major internal transformation. In the Wizard of Oz, the Tinman represents civilization's mechanical side during the Great Depression. The Tinman wants a heart so he can feel love, and that is what he wants; what he needs is a human touch, a reconnection with his emotional side.

There's a difference between what a character wants and needs; needs are more about internal transformation and reassembling the broken or missing pieces of oneself. Let's find out what wants are.

HOW TO KNOW WHAT YOUR CHARACTER WANTS

Independent of the character's needs, what they want comes from an external source. There are many ways a person with no self-worth or confidence in themselves can try and find value, but it only ends up returning to just a few important things: money, power, love, and respect. What Your Character wants almost always boils down to something physical, emotional, or mental; they're trying hard to find some external solution to fix their inner brokenness. What the character wants is nearly always wrong for them and what the character needs is nearly almost subconscious. For example, the protagonist may want the most beautiful but bitchy girl in school, but he needs a pleasant girl who treats him respectfully.

YOUR CHARACTER MEETS THEIR GHOST

There is a Ghost in your Character's past that haunts them—for Simba; it's his guilt; for Scrooge, it's his mean spirit, foreshadowed by the ghost of Jacob Marley; for Macbeth, it is guilt in the form of Banquo's spirit, and so on. Sometimes the metaphorical ghost is used to symbolize what haunts the protagonist.

The ghosts are past baggage: wounds from the past, painful childhood memories, a traumatic experience, a disastrous relationship, guilt, shame, or embarrassment—anything that changes a character's personality or perspective or encumbers their present self is a ghost that needs to be addressed in the plot. This feeling infects every aspect of their life, and they feel there is no release for someone like them who hasn't been able or willing to make amends for the past acts until some other person's intervention, some event, conflict, or ordeal exposes this lie.

So what makes this ghost a rubric for character development? No matter how much peering intellect, wisdom, or foresight your protagonist is blessed with, they must be irked by these ghosts to the extent of toiling and tormenting their inner selves to evolve. And achieve that end, make the ghost as big and unforgettable as possible. The larger the demons, the greater the victory over them!

MOMENT OF YOUR CHARACTER'S JOURNEY

Now that you have carved out the lies, the ghosts, the wants vis-a-vis the needs of your character, it's time for them to launch into their life struggle, that is, the action of the plot. When your protagonist steps out into the spotlight for their big start, they are unstoppable. For instance, let's look at Oedipus:

- His ghost: the prophecy he would kill his father and marry his mother
- His lies: he could change his destiny
- His want: to answer the sphynx's questions, prove his intellect, and later become a worthy king for his people by getting to the heart of the matter—what is the reason of the curse
- His needs: self-knowledge and truth, which change his world (internal and external) forever

When you have created this four-pronged structure for your character, you are ready to launch them into the thick of things. The next part of their journey through the different plot points will be hinged on these pillars.

THE DILEMMA OF THE NORMAL WORLD

Character introduction is one of the most vital moments in your story and should always be followed up by some context from the 'normal world.' The normal world is a place of comfort in which your character has found momentary comfort or contentment. Maybe they are happy with their life, or perhaps it's just easy for them to remain complacent as things stand now, but this state will not last forever! The Normal World provides a reference point for all of these changes. Taking the example of Oedipus Rex again, the place where Oedipus is in life in the 'now' of the play—the King of Thebes, with a wife and subjects who look up to him—is an excellent place to be in, despite the recent challenges of the plague that the kingdom is faced with. This calm before the storm or 'high station' in life makes the sting of the fall more bitter when tragedy strikes.

BEGINNING OF THE FIRST ACT

The first act is the most crucial part of any story. It sets the stage for what's going to happen and how it all begins—introducing all the main characters and their problems (lies and ghosts) or goals (wants and needs) in life, the setting for their story to unfold, and the atmosphere of momentary 'normalcy.' All this prepares the reader and keeps them engaged to follow through to 'what next.

Introduce all characters who are vital catalysts for conflict and provide some insight into their predicaments and agenda: the protagonist's personal struggles, external conflicts, and potential opponents/opposing forces trying to keep them from their goals. The main storyline is established here—the hero's internal struggle vis-a-vis overcoming external obstacles.

TWIST OF THE FIRST PLOT POINT

The point in the first act, when everything changes, is "the beginning of the conflict." This is the point of no return where the real action begins. From this point on, the story becomes more exciting and engaging. The first plot point occurs after around 20-25% of your reading—the character is now set to leave the ordinary world as the story takes an unexpected turn. It's a significant scene that sets the tone for what will happen from here onwards; it's the crucial moment that tells that from now onwards, the character's life will no longer be the same. For instance, the train from platform no. 9 3/4 does not only take Harry to Hogwarts; it takes him to the destiny he was born to fulfill.

WHAT HAPPENS IN THE FIRST HALF OF THE SECOND ACT

The first half of the second act is where your character has their world turned upside down and gets lost. When the old rules no longer apply, you start to see things differently. Here, the character puts themself in a trying situation. They are at their wit's end when losing what they want seems imminent. Your character will experience intense, passionate emotions during this time. They are learning which methods are ineffective for achieving their goals, and sometimes, also what their actual goals are. We can call it the pre-midpoint rising action. An example would be when Elizabeth in *Pride and Prejudice,* after turning down Collins's marriage proposal in Wickham's departure, visits her friend Charlotte and meets Mr. Darcy, about whom she had already decided not to like again.

THE TURNING POINT

The failures in the first half of the act will have the protagonist reevaluate their life, and they will start to figure out what's important. Slowly, even subconsciously, they are learning new things about themselves, distinguishing wants and needs, and getting a better self-understanding until finally, they arrive at their moment of truth halfway through the story. The midpoint is about the protagonist shift, where the character is pushed to engage in the core of the conflict. And that necessary push comes from raised stakes. The protagonist realizes the actual danger of the opponent's intentions due to their own failure. In *Harry Potter and the Philosopher's Stone,* the midpoint is Harry's realization that someone is trying to steal the stone for Voldemort and that if they fail to protect it, it will have dire consequences—make Voldemort stronger.

THE INTERESTING SECOND HALF OF THE SECOND ACT

The second half of the second act is where your character shifts from the reactive phase into the active one. They start taking control of themselves at this stage. Learning the truth at the midpoint allowed them to start implementing corrective actions in their quest for their goal. Thanks to the significant personal revelation achieved during this phase, they see why things are happening the way they are and how best to tackle the course of action.

THE THIRD PLOT POINT - ULTIMATE TRUTH?

At the end of the second act, our protagonist steers close to victory, but everything is thrown off course in the third plot point. The third plot point introduces an obstacle or potential threat within a perfect opportunity for success that hinders the protagonist's plans. When Harry encounters Quirrel and realizes it was Voldemort, all the while acting like a parasite, is a moment when all his plans seem unhinged for a moment.

At this point, the protagonist seems helpless for a moment. However, the protagonist finds another way! Going back to the Potter instance, once he knows from looking into the Mirror of Ersid that the stone was always in his pocket, Harry finds a way to defend it.

Such events either force the character to admit that everything they believed was wrong or, as in Harry's case, realize that they are worthy of a lot more and more robust than they could ever imagine. In short, they get cured of the lies and the ghosts.

EXPLORE THE FIRST HALF OF THE THIRD ACT

The beginning of the third act is all about your character's scramble to regain balance before facing off with the antagonist in the climactic scene.

The Third Act of any story concerns the main Character's internal journey. It's a time when he faces questions about what it means to serve the truth and if that price is worth paying for them to find peace at long last. The confrontation scene between Po and Tai-Lung in Kung Fu Panda over the Dragon Scroll is orchestrated around the realization that 'there's no secret ingredient'—the truth which Po discovers (need) and hence becomes the Dragon Warrior (want). After this point, the character is never going back into the lie again—their transformation is complete.

THE MOST AWAITED CLIMAX

Your Character has been through a lot, but they are more seasoned at the end. This final push helps them see that life can be better outside of what's comfortable or routine, to do something more meaningful for themselves and others. The audience has witnessed the transformation from the inside out, as the 'lies' are replaced with truth, and we arrive at a moment of clarity.

The protagonist has been fighting a pitched battle with the antagonistic force for some time now. There is tension in this scene that is unbearable, and it's about to break out into violence once again! This is a crucial moment when the audience is excited, nervous, and hungry for what will happen at the end.

BUILDING THE RESOLUTION

It's always a good idea to end on an exciting note so your readers don't get bored and want more. The audience now knows that the character lived in his ordinary world, as shaped by the lie. The resolution is the character's new world, where he can always find peace and happiness —the happily ever after the audience was rooting for all this while!

The success of a positive character arc lies in the feeling that the reader, along with your protagonist, has come out alive at the end of this story. Their faith in humanity is restored after experiencing something terrible through the first-hand experience of a character they could relate with. By allowing your character the moments of vulnerability through the lies they lived and the ghosts that haunt them, you add a human element that enlists the reader's empathy and involvement.

CREATIVE EXERCISES TO PRACTICE

When creating a character, it's essential to consider the thematic elements they will demonstrate throughout your story. For these plot points and themes to resonate with each other entertainingly, see if you can identify qualities already possessed by your protagonist. Answering these equations will give you an in-depth understanding of what your character's journey will look like.

Answers these questions about your Character:

Q1. Can you come up with some minor characters that can play a part as the catalyst to encourage your protagonist?

Q2. How did the Character come through inner conflict despite the Ghost being massive and it was difficult to turn into a hero? Craft the journey from Ghost to Hero!

____

____

____

____

____

____

Q3. How was Midpoint a turning highlight in the Character's life?

____

____

____

____

____

Q4. Write how the Character discovered his true potential and at which stage/stages.

____

____

____

____

____

____

Q5. State the connection between Character and climax!

____

____

____

____

____

CHAPTER 2
THE FLAT ARC

Remember how we distinguished between two character types, round and flat—a round character undergoes change while a flat character remains the same from beginning to end. A character who evolves through the different crucial points in the plot and becomes a better version of themselves is a round character with a positive arc. But what about those characters who do not change and never learn from their mistakes, but it still brings them happiness in some form or another? Take the example of Diana from *Wonder Woman*. She can be considered a character with a flat arc because, from the inception to the end, she is a firm believer in the power of love to truly save this world. Her conviction even convinces the soldier steve Trevor and brings an end to the world war.

So you see that the protagonist in a flat arc is constantly changing the world around them rather than being changed by it. In contrast, in stories featuring round characters or those with a change arc, we see an individual's life change dramatically for better or worse, and then that event is used as motivation for whatever follows in the character's journey. In this type of narrative structure featuring a flat character, however, there isn't really any particular "next thing" happening until much later on down the road.

THE TRUTH YOUR CHARACTER BELIEVES

A character with a flat arc does not have any lies; instead, there is a predominant 'truth,' a conviction, a belief, or a prevalent character trait that guides their journey and modulates the pace and movement of the story to a great extent. No matter what happens in the character's life, that truth remains unshaken. Even the antagonists sometimes can take the upper hand over the main character, fully understanding their consistency or unchangeability. Take the example of Batman (or any superhero for that matter after they become superheroes, that is, after discovering their superpowers) from the second installment of Christopher Nolan's Batman trilogy, *The Dark Knight.* Nolan has portrayed both his protagonist and the antagonist—Batman and the Joker—as classic cases of flat characters. While the Joker's predominant trait is chaos and anarchy, Batman's truth is the belief in the essential goodness of people and people's belief in genuine goodness. To preserve that truth, he even sacrifices himself, taking the blame for everything that went wrong in Gotham, thus absolving Harvey Dent (ironically the only round central character in the movie) after he had gone rogue and died. Batman sacrifices his image and chooses to be the dark Knight to keep people's faith in goodness, symbolized by Harvey's clean image. That's how a flat character arc remains unchanged by external circumstances. More than the outer darkness, these characters are guided by their inner light, which is never dimmed.

This flat arc protagonist is a shaman who has found the Truth and will use this power to save not just themselves but also everyone else. They might even change our world for good in Lie-burdened times!

Exercise 1: Can you explain any 3 variations of the truth and specify them?

____

____

____

____

____

____

Exercise 2: You are about to embark on a journey that will shape your Character and thus write any one variable that will be the primary truth of the character. Choose wisely from the 3 variations mentioned above.

____

____

____

____

____

THE NORMAL WORLD

The protagonist in a story always has to face some kind of challenge—a threat to their beliefs/convictions, a danger to the lives of those they hold dear. To cut a long story short, this challenge always comes as a potential blow to destabilize their ordinary world. The character responds by fighting for what's 'right' against all odds (like when your favorite character goes up against an evil empire) or even just trying not to be lost among other people who are also trying their best but failing anyway.

This will set the stage for the story to follow.

Exercise 1: Let's start with creating a Normal World for your character. Write down how you would best describe this world and how it will be the most suitable choice for the character's arc.

____

____

____

____

____

____

The protagonist's world, or what they know of it, could be a good place representing truth for them in their life—as the ordinary world does at the first plot point. Unless something happens and forces the character out of their comfort zone, chances of any kind of action from a character etched on the flat arc are lean since they are already securely and firmly rooted in their truths. The question is, how long in the plot do we wait to introduce this complication in the ordinary world?

The protagonist finds themself in a less-than-satisfactory world, with nothing but their truth to guide them on the journey of escape or building better worlds. For Hamlet, it's the blood-tainted state of Denmark; for Bruce Wayne, it's the city of Gotham swallowed by organized crime.

Their battle against all odds can either make them stronger in what they already believed in, as in the case of the Batman, because now they're fighting not just for themselves but also for everyone else that's suffering under these altered circumstances. They must win at any cost! Or, their predominant nature or truth drives them towards a self-destructive extreme where they lose their lives but succeed in establishing some kind of order, as we see in the case of Hamlet.

Exercise 1: Let's assume that there is an ordinary world that you have described but can you now also write down your unique version of this storyline?

____

____

____

____

____

Exercise 2: Describe the physical settings of the ordinary world.

THE CHARACTERISTIC MOMENT

What makes your flat arc protagonist unique is that they're not exactly like you and me. They have skills, abilities, or habits that make them extraordinary. Maybe it's their size (or lack thereof), appearance, personality trait(s), or superpower(s). So the first thing you must know about your protagonist is what sets them apart from the general humanity. But besides that, there are a few other details that you must jot down t help you with a detailed character portrayal.

Exercise 1: Let's now discover the best characteristic moment for your character in the flat arc version! Also, can you answer these questions?

Question 1: Name of your character?

____

____

Question 2: Estimated age of your character?

____

____

____

Question 3: Nationality of your character (Where did the parents originate)

____

____

____

____

Question 4: Your Character's occupation or some traits that can define his primary identity? (Businessman, brilliant, rebel, high on self-esteem).

____

____

____

Question 5: Define your character's physical characteristics (e.g., Birthmark, injury).

____

____

____

Question 6: Explain any 4 personality traits of your character that can best describe him and help readers connect with him. (Kind, gentlemen, witty, angry, likable).

____

____

____

Question 7: What is that one vital personality trait, skill or virtue that best describes or exemplifies the character?

____

____

____

Question 8: Find the connection here! Write down how you would like your readers to sympathize with your character. How will they engage with him?

____

____

____

Question 9: Write down your character's overall story!

____

____

____

Question 10: There is always a contrast between the Protagonist and lie-hidden characters. How will you overdo the contrast and keep your readers hooked?

____

____

____

Question 11: Does your character have any scene expectations in the opening chapter?

____

____

____

Question 12: Now think deeply. Whatever you have written about your character, will this help know your readers about the character's truth?

____

____

____

Question 13: Now, can you define the ghost since you are now aware of the truth?

____

____

____

Question 14: Now, can you make your character so enjoyable that the readers fall in love with it? Or maybe they discover some sort of connection with him?

____

____

____

Question 15: Write down your character's strengths.

____

____

____

Question 16: Write down your character's weaknesses.

Exercise 2: Can you think of some over-the-top drama to help introduce your character in the first chapter? Keep it engaging and interactive so that readers are amazed. Describe certain events and find answers from the above exercises.

Exercise 3: Now, go on to write a summary of the first introductory chapter and notice that your character has a memorable moment.

Exercise 4: After summarising your Characteristic Moment, review the following checklist to discover how effective your choice of scenes will be.

- Introduced character?

- Revealed the character's name and age?

- Indicated character's gender and physical attributes

- Indicated character's existing personality traits, occupation, industry he belongs to, and identity

- Indicated character's nationality

- List down significant physical characteristics

- Write down the role in the story

- Taken care of the reader's sympathy, expectations, and interest

- Described a story goal

- Developed a Lie

THE FIRST ACT

The first quarter of a flat arc story sets the stage for what's to come. So you need an intriguing hook, exciting conflict, and engaging characters to keep the readers involved.

The first choice you have to make is to decide the extent of the 'lie' or challenges working in cross-purposes with the character's truth. The protagonist can always discover what is at stake for them if the lie isn't overthrown—mostly, it is the normalcy of their 'normal world' (and all those who live in that world) that can be compromised if the lie wins over or coexists with their convictions of truth. For example, if the Joker lies that deep down, everyone in Gotham is ugly and, if given an opportunity, will kill others to secure their own lives win, then the soul of Gotham will be compromised. Hence, Batman's truth that goodness and people's faith in acts of goodness have to be preserved. The character's truth encompasses the fate of many around them. In a flat arc, characters' restless pursuit of defending their truth (at the price of staying unchanged throughout the story) always takes on a higher purpose, a goal more significant than their own development as a person/character, sometimes as grand as the impact of the actions of an epic hero.

THE FIRST PLOT POINT

The First Act ends with this significant scene where the stage is set for the lie threatening the normalcy of the protagonist's world. Now, it's time for some significant changes! There will be a seemingly easy path to follow if the protagonist sticks to their convictions/truth, even at the expense of alienating his community/people who populate his 'normal world.' The readers will soon find out how high the stakes are as these inhabitants of the character's ordinary world are doomed to a tryst with the fortune-altering 'lie, or challenge.

THE FIRST HALF OF THE SECOND ACT

Unlike the positive arc change, the flat arc character will spend the first half of the second act being punished for believing in their truth. They will be surrounded by people who try to convince them that their beliefs are wrong. But, if they genuinely believe in the truth, then this is a challenge they must face against all odds! It is an actual test of the character's integrity and resilience—how far they can go to defend their convictions, and at what cost? Could it be that everyone else is right and their faith has been misplaced? Maybe the Truth is really a lie and vice versa!

This moment of indecisiveness is the characteristic predicament faced by a flat character with a positive trajectory. However, they never abandon their truth. In the case of a flat character with a negative trajectory, like the Joker, the belief/truth is unshakeable from beginning to end. Another epic instance of a flat character is Milton's Satan in Paradise Lost. Though in the later books, he loses his verve and his 'false heroism' becomes too apparent, Satan remains faithful to his truth, despite which side of the moral arc he is placed.

Exercise: Now answer the questions that are context to the First Half of the story up till the second act.

Question 1: What and how will you oppose the antagonist's Lie with the help of tools that your character will receive?

____

____

____

____

____

Question 2: How will you show the truth through your character to others instead of just telling them? Have you thought of any particular scene?

____

____

____

____

____

Question 3: How is your Protagonist feeling slightly out of place within the new Adventure World of the Second Act?

____

____

____

____

Question 4: What will you do if your Protagonist is still trying to reach his goal via truth-based actions?

____

____

____

____

THE MIDPOINT

This is where you can really take your time and make sure everything's perfect. The midpoint comes after the protagonist has experienced some epiphany or revelation, which provides them with new information about themselves or others that changes their perspective! However, for a flat arc, this change isn't a 360-degree shift in perspective because that's the journey for a round character. In a flat arc, the revelation/epiphany is either a reconfirmation of the character's truth or a new way to arrive at it that was not accessible or visible to them. In short, the character embarks on a feasible solution to external problems/challenges/lies. They finally understand what all this has been about in a flash of insight.

At the midpoint of their journey, your protagonist must face a momentous decision. But this redemptive event isn't offered to him as an opportunity for growth and change; instead, it comes at a high personal cost. The protagonist offers truth to everyone else. Allies that were previously resisting can see what's going on and start following positive change arcs of their own!

Exercise: Now answer these questions at your story's Midpoint where character involvement just gets more interesting.

Question 1: Write down your story's exact event where the table will turn at the Midpoint.

____

____

____

____

____

____

Question 2: Write how you will help readers understand this scene as much as possible. What will be your approach?

____

____

____

____

Question 3: The events of the midpoint are likely to prompt a moment where our protagonist must make an important decision, which will either allow him to continue on with his journey in peace. How will you describe this event?

____

____

____

____

____

Question 4: How will these prompt minor characters to turn away from the effects of a Lie in their lives?

\
\
\
\
\
\

Question 5: Write down the names of 3 or 4 characters that will arise at the Midpoint. Some essential characters around the Protagonist.

THE SECOND HALF OF THE SECOND ACT

The midpoint changes everything in the plot. Doubts are replaced by confidence and reaffirmation of the character's beliefs as they continue their journey toward the resolution. They are not going to back down from this fight. If anything, they are more committed and determined than ever before!

The protagonist has seen through the lies/challenges and has determined to use this knowledge for their benefit. As a result, their aggressive actions in the section will dramatically affect their and everyone else's fate around them. The Second Act ends with a definitive victory, but it's really a setup for imminent defeat at the third plot point.

Exercise 1: Answer the following questions in context to the story in the Second Half of the Second Act.

Question 1: Can you describe the state of mind or explain how the character is reacting at the Midpoint and what is the conflict now?

____

____

____

____

____

____

Question 2: Now that the 'Moment of Truth is out, what are the new tools that your character will use?

Question 3: What is the existence of lies now in the Protagonist's life, and is it still a threat to him?

Question 4: When the Protagonist is stuck between the truth and the lie, what will the world around him look like? Can you describe some situational events here?

THE THIRD PLOT POINT

Your character faces their greatest fear; they will be vulnerable and broken. They may come to terms with the truth about themselves or figure out how much more robust than everyone else in this world they really are—it's debatable! But all of these things lead towards a new resolve, one where they are ready again to fight against whatever awaits ahead without flinching.

When the character has a flat arc, it's up to them how they respond—if they succeed in defending their truth over lies or die trying. So make your third plot point as personal and accurate to the character as possible to make it a natural outcome of who this character essentially is.

THE FIRST HALF OF THE THIRD ACT

The Protagonist is in a tight spot, but they still haven't given up hope. The first half of the third act will focus on how they survive and proceed from there, with every remaining resource at their disposal for planning the next move.

The Protagonist is left with one last chance to hit the antagonistic force. Since this segment will be comparatively quiet and thoughtful, you can give them another opportunity to debate which was the right side to defend—truth or lie? This internal debate gives better clarity about what really matters.

THE CLIMAX

The climax is the most exciting part of your story, of all stories for that matter! It's where you finally take all the buildup in the third act to the highest point of rising action—from where it's a downward arc towards resolution, speaking plot-wise. As far as the character arc is concerned, the climax is the elastic limit to which every character, round or flat, is tested in a story. The protagonist will have to face their greatest challenge, that is, the final attempt of the lies of an opposing force to entrap the character. They do this depending on whether it's a positive change arc or not, but one thing remains true for both: the character's truth (no matter on which side of the moral curve it places them) always prevails over a lie!

The climax of a flat arc is basically a moment of reconfirmation of the character's truth. The protagonist is relentless in pursuing their goals; the antagonistic force can no longer sway their resolve now that their truth is reconfirmed. When Harry discovers the philosopher's stone in his own pocket, and Voldemort, sheltered in Quirrel, tries to entice him to join hands and do extraordinary things together, the temptation is not strong enough to win over the eleven-year-old wizard who always chose the 'right thing' over the easy thing to do.

So the main character faces the most difficult challenge in the climax. This is often followed by supporting characters facing similar tests to determine their dedication toward truth and goodness in general. More significant the predicament, the more satisfactory the resolution.

Exercise: Answer the following questions about your character's Climax in the story.

Question 1: Get ready because you now have to write about the ultimate confrontation between the Antagonistic force and the Protagonist take?

Question 2: Where exactly will your Climax happen or take place?

____

____

____

____

____

____

Question 3: Can you describe the nature of your ultimate climax and the confrontation? How will the Protagonist's truth fight against antagonistic force?

____

____

____

____

____

Question 4: What is that event or moment that the readers were waiting for until now? Have you thought of that one moment? Think like a reader here.

____

____

____

____

____

____

____

THE RESOLUTION

The Resolution is where the conflict reaches its peak, and everything changes for good. In a flat arc, these moments will be most evident in the change manifested in the supporting cast members or the aspects of the world around the protagonist. All the lies finally fade away as the character's truth is firmly established, not just for them but for the community/people who feature in their world. The supporting characters who have been fighting to believe in the truth are now fighting for it and will be the protagonist's allies in not just restoring but maintaining the normalcy of their world.

Exercise: Answer the following questions now.

Question 1: What is your character about to do next since the external conflict is now over? Have you thought of this?

____

____

____

____

____

Question 2: Think about the Resolution and answer how you can best describe the settings of the Resolution.

____

____

____

____

____

____

Question 3: In the story, we are introduced to a new ordinary world that's better than what came before. What four ways can you think of which would contrast this?

____

____

____

____

____

____

Question 4: The Protagonist has inspired four minor characters to take a stand against their old ways of living. Each one's story is unique, and they all share some commonalities. Can you name them and describe how they have changed now? Any differences from then till now?

____

____

____

Question 5: Can you answer this Thematic question in the first chapter based on the Resolution?

Question 6: How will your final scene be an upbeat one that demonstrates the hope of a new and better day dawning for the Protagonist's world?

____

____

____

____

____

____

CREATIVE EXERCISES

Describe the truth your character believes in, in just one or two sentences. And then go on to expand it into your story's thematic questions.

The question is that you have to highlight the question in the story. It can be either mild or massive. Then, you must decide which one you are willing to follow in the protagonist's way.

Something to focus on here:

1. There must be an event where the Protagonist first becomes aware of the Lie's existence and the threat. Can you describe this event and everything about this?

2. What is the character's motivation for overcoming a certain obstacle in his quest? Is it because he needs to defeat Lie, or will that happen automatically as part of achieving other goals along the way?

3. The Lie is a powerful tool in the First Act. How can you use it to your advantage?

____

____

____

____

____

____

4. How will the protagonist's enemies, who are already deeply embedded in lies, become even more deranged?

____

____

____

____

____

CHAPTER 3

THE NEGATIVE CHANGE ARC TYPE 1: DISILLUSIONMENT

Everybody looks forward to a happy ending, but it doesn't happen for everyone!

The power of negative change arcs is unparalleled. These stories resonate with audiences emotionally, creating immersive experiences that transport one into another world or even deeper into the alleys of the human mind! The more complicated a truth, the more critical it is to comprehend.

Change arcs illustrate how characters change throughout their stories. There is no "right" answer to the question of whether or not your character should have a negative arc or a positive one, as every character is a manifestation of its own choices and personality traits which evolve over time through different plot twists and conflicts. It is possible that the character's trajectory goes from bad to worse, stuck on an endless loop, trying desperately to find their way out.

While the disillusionment arc certainly has its negative aspects, it also offers a learning curve for the character. As with any positive change in life, there are always new discoveries that push us towards becoming better versions of ourselves; the negative change arc, too, has its set of takeaways.

THE LIE YOUR CHARACTER BELIEVES

As in a positive change arc, the disillusionment arc tells that the character is living a lie and is ignorant of it. The disillusionment with the lie seems to cost them their health—physical, mental, emotional—and happiness because the new truth is tragic. The Greek tragedy *Oedipus Rex* is a classic demonstration of the negative character arc. Oedipus believes his lie—that his efforts to avert the prophecy about him killing his father and marrying his mother by leaving Corinth have been successful. But fate brings him to Thebes, his actual birthplace, and on the way, he kills an unknown stranger in the heat of the moment who, coincidentally, was his birth father and the king of Thebes. Thebes, now captured by the Sphynx in the absence of the king, is delivered by Oedipus as he successfully answers the riddles of the Sphynx and becomes the king. He also marries the queen, not knowing that she was his birth mother. So, when Oedipus's relentless pursuit of a different truth—how to save Thebes from the clasp of the plague—ends in his normal world's collapse, he meets the tragic end of self-blinding. However, you must understand that not so much does Oedipus's character have a change arc but his circumstances.

Whether internal or external, the change marks a negative end for the character with a disillusionment arc.

Exercise 1: Can you describe the 5 variations that will help your character believe in the Lie? All these variations should be specific and easy to understand.

____

____

____

____

____

____

Exercise 2: Now write down the primary Lie which will play a significant role in deciding your character's arc. Pick one from the 5 variations that you have stated above. Consider everything, and then cast your plot and theme based on that Lie's influence.

____

____

____

____

____

Exercise 3: The character's Lie is an empty space that he has been trying to fill for years. His exterior world reflects this inner struggle, with nothing filling up those vacancies and only hardship in return. Now you can find those three ways that will go about describing how his life might look.

____

____

____

____

____

____

THE THING YOUR CHARACTER NEEDS

Disillusionment arcs can be seen as a way to show the audience that what they believe may not actually exist. The character comes into contact with their own truth—their need—which sets them free from anything holding them back or preventing growth, though the impact of that moment of clarity is primarily devastating. For instance, Macbeth's ambitions were a lie when he realizes how he has lost every-thing in that pursuit—Lady Macbeth goes insane, and most impor-tantly, he is haunted by the ghosts of his own guilt. He realizes the price he had to pay to pursue his ambition (want)—his peace of mind (need).

The end of Macbeth's lies coincides with the end of Macbeth himself, so the question is how and when the character grows after the disillusionment. On second thought, it is the growth or change arc that makes the disillusionment possible.

Exercise: Answer the following questions now. These questions are in context to the Thing Your Character Needs.

Question 1: Explain the Truth vs Lie that your character believes in.

____

____

____

____

____

____

____

____

____

Question 2: What are the five ways your story's truth can manifest as something that the character needs? This will be an action or belief they have.

____

____

____

____

____

____

____

____

____

____

____

____

Question 3: What will the world look like at this point?

THE THING YOUR CHARACTER WANTS

What's the one thing your character wants? What is their central story goal, and how do they go about achieving a way that seems both reasonable (based upon false perceptions) yet also worthy?

For example, the character of Nick Carraway in The Great Gatsby makes the error of confusing his needs with his wants. His midwestern upbringing and general naivete make him believe that the rich and famous are precisely who they are, that the lives of the residents of East egg were perfectly happy, and hence, he is deluded into desiring to become one of them. That's his want or lie. What he actually needs is the knowledge of the truth behind their surface glitz and glamour, an insight into the shallowness of their facades of 'happiness.'

Such half-truths or incomplete knowledge of the nature of things mislead the characters, and they stray further from the truth or what they actually need. However, as the story progresses, they realize what really matters in life, and that realization can be heartbreaking or tragic.

Exercise 1: Write down four possible things your character wants. What desires drive you to take on this adventure? What is your character's deepest wish that they strive for in the story? These are not necessarily their primary goal, but they will influence what purpose he or she pursues throughout each chapter.

Exercise 2: The best way to write a story is by determining what your main character wants and then determining how they will get it. For this process not only to work but also feel satisfying as well-you need an objective plot goal that can guide every decision made throughout the entire piece of writing!

THE CHARACTERISTIC MOMENT

The characteristic moment is the essence of your protagonist's character arc. It launches them into their journey and defines how the reader/audience views them throughout the piece. The reader is made to ask themselves some vital questions at this point: do they empathize with this character? Does the character's predicament or their 'lies' seem relatable? What would the reader/audience do if pitted against or under similar circumstances?

The characteristic moment of the protagonist is that crucial moment when their predominant traits—both negative and positive ones—shine out. In the case of Macbeth, Act I, scene iii is that characteristic moment—the audience is acquainted with his military prowess and his fatal ambition through his first encounter with the three witches. The entire scene is like a premonition to an inevitable catastrophe that his 'ambition' will let loose.

This characteristic moment binds the reader in an abiding contract of staying a witness to the ups and downs in this character's life hereafter in the book/story; the possibilities for Disillusionment to come later on down the road.

Exercise #1: The character you create in your story must have a specific set of characteristics. To do this, answer these questions:

- What is the main trait that defines them?
- What are their most prominent features and habits like as people?
- For example, do they have any special abilities such as super strength but are also afraid to go to school because there's always an expectation put upon us by society about how we should behave when given specific opportunities?

____

____

____

____

____

____

____

____

____

____

Question 1: Can you describe the character's role here in the story? If he is in the main lead as a Protagonist or Antagonist? Is he a mentor, supporting character, or someone else?

____

____

____

Question 2: Estimated age of your character?

____

____

____

Question 3: Nationality of your character (exciting, right?)

____

____

____

Question 4: Your Character's occupation or some traits that can define his primary identity? (Businessman, intelligent, rebellious, high on self-esteem.)

____

____

____

____

____

Question 5: Define your character's physical characteristics (e.g., Birthmark, injury).

____

____

____

____

____

Question 6: Explain any 4 personality traits of your character that can best describe him and help readers connect with him. (Kind, gentlemen, witty, angry, likable).

____

____

____

____

Question 7: Describe one crucial personality trait of your character that best explains him. Talk about its virtues or skill or anything that you think is an essential yet impactful trait.

____

____

____

____

____

Question 8: How can you help readers connect with him through sympathy, relatability, or anything interesting? Try to find a connection here.

____

____

____

____

____

Question 9: Explain the story goal of your character along with What does he want the most? 'That Thing,' focus on it.

Question 10: Now, can you make your character so enjoyable that the readers fall in love with it? Or maybe they discover some sort of relatability with him?

Question 11: Write down your character's strengths.

Question 12: Write down your character's weaknesses.

Question 10: Describe the character's scene goal at the start of the chapter.

____

____

____

Question 12: Can you demonstrate a scene where you portray the character's Lie? Some sort of hint for the readers?

____

____

____

____

Exercise 2: What if the answers to all of your questions were dramatic, exciting, and had characters in motion? You could use this as an opening scene for a story or novel! Try coming up with four different events that will create curiosity.

____

____

____

Exercise 3: In the opening chapter, you will be introduced to a well-rounded and diverse group of characters. Write down about those individual personalities through memorable Characteristic Moments that show how they are distinctive from one another in both good ways as well as bad ones!

Exercise 4: Think of the opening scene as a whole, but break it up into smaller pieces to make more sense. You might want or need two scenes, for example, one where your main character meets someone and another that follows their innermost thoughts before they arrive at this eventful meeting.

____

____

____

____

____

____

____

____

____

THE NORMAL WORLD

The characteristic moment gives readers an understanding of the character, but it's not enough on its own. The everyday world provides context for what makes them tick and how they interact within that setting and shows us their place in society or groupthink wars; we need this information so our feelings about these characters can develop and we can decide how and how much to align with the character!

The Normal World is where your character has found contentment or complacency; for characters with a disillusionment arc, it is also the cradle of their lies. It's an essential element in grounding the first act of any story, setting the stage for the rising action.

Macbeth's normal world is a universe of moral uncertainty where the protagonist is solely guided by his ambition, and the opening scene with the three witches sets the tone for the universe the audience is going to venture into, even before the introduction of the protagonist. The normal world is a universe with its own set of rules and standards to live up to—the character either lives up to those 'rules' or dies trying as, for a disillusioned arc character, this normal world is designed as a setting for the impending disillusionment.

Let's take the opening of One Flew Over The Cuckoo's Nest as another example. What type of change can you see happening to your character in this story, and how does it affect them later on? It's essential for every arc, no matter what kind (problem / resolution), to have a learning curve for the character. There will be nothing but blandness throughout all subsequent parts without these vivid openings!

Exercise: Answer the following questions in context to the Normal World in your story.

Question 1: Can you describe the exterior setting of the Normal World? Some sort of physical setting?

____

____

____

____

____

____

Question 2: What does your chosen Normal World symbolically represent?

____

____

____

____

____

Question 3: Write down to show the Protagonist's "before" state; what would happen to him in his Normal World? What happened when he first woke up and saw where it was that now felt unfamiliar?

____

____

____

____

____

Question 4: What is the most logical backstory for your character's belief in a lie?

____

____

____

____

____

Question 5: What has prevented the protagonist from leaving his normal world now?

____

____

____

____

Question 6: Your character is being empowered by the Normal World, which gives him no reason to question his lie. Why is this happening?

____

____

____

____

Question 7: The Normal World is a world of stability, with rules and limitations. The Adventure World has no boundaries or barriers- anything can happen anytime! Write down the contrast between the two.

____

____

____

____

____

Question 8: The Adventure World of your story's central conflict is filled with nail-biting danger, heart-pounding excitement, and hair-raising terrors. Explain this event.

____

____

____

____

Question 9: When your Protagonist is later forced out of the Normal World into the Second Act, how will this change his beliefs about what's real and fake?

____

____

———————————————————————————————

———————————————————————————————

———————————————————————————————

Question 10: Answer if the character will return to the Normal World at the end of the story.

———————————————————————————————

———————————————————————————————

———————————————————————————————

———————————————————————————————

THE FIRST ACT

The disillusionment arc is about the protagonist overcoming their lie, or in this case, believing a lovely and idealistic truth. That's why the discovery that things weren't quite what they seemed at first glance leaves them unhinged; instead of being empowered by finally seeing through the lies their ordinary world has presented to them all their life, they end up more confused than ever, knowing not how to cope with this altered reality.

Exercise: Answer the following questions on the First Act of your story.

Question 1: Can you dramatize the character's Lie to create some severe thrill about it? An excellent hook for the readers?

____

____

____

____

____

Question 2: Show the character's contentment in the Lie and his real or idealistic view of the world.

____

____

____

____

____

Question 3: Write how you will show or present the Thing Your Character Wants and Needs.

____

____

____

____

____

____

Question 4: Can you write that part where the character in the Characteristic Moment gets a hint about the Lie?

____

____

____

____

____

Question 5: The Lie will be readily evident in his Normal World, but how would you show that in the story?

Question 6: What are some ways you can reinforce the Lie throughout the First Act? State any 4 ways.

Question 7: Can you hint about the character's inability with the truth and throw some light on the same?

____

____

____

____

____

____

THE FIRST PLOT POINT

For an unhappy ending to resonate, the readers must be prepared for it. They should see this as the only logical outcome and that there's no other way in which things could have turned out differently for the character.

Exercise: Answer the following questions about the First Plot Point in your story.

Question 1: So you know that the character has left the Normal World, what should be that event when this takes place? Explain that central conflict.

____

____

____

Question 2: How are you planning to make this event exciting for readers?

____

____

____

____

Question 3: Can you choose which of the following best describes the First Plot Point? Something extremely positive or vulnerable?

____

____

____

Question 4: What decision did your character make that led him up to the First Plot Point, taking at least partial responsibility for what happens?

____

____

____

____

____

Question 5: How can you best describe your First Plot Point?

____

____

____

____

____

____

Question 6: The main character's reaction to the First Plot Point will determine how they approach conflict in the Second Act but what would be the reaction? Describe this in detail to understand the track of the arc.

____

____

____

____

____

____

Question 7: Just after the First Plot Point, what can be those tentative physical needs of your character that he must be looking at? Can you name them?

____

____

____

____

Question 8: What new direction will the character take now that they have achieved their goal?

____

____

____

____

____

____

____

THE FIRST HALF OF THE SECOND ACT

The character is getting farther away from what they need while pursuing what they want.

A disillusionment arc happens when someone who was once idealistic about their goals has an epiphany that makes them realize the futility of their entire situation, triggering emotional trauma as there's no turning back now no matter how desperately they want to.

Exercise: Answer the following questions about the First Half of the Second Act in your story.

Question 1: What event or series of events will cause your character to see the cracks in his lies?

____

____

____

____

____

____

Question 2: The protagonist is struggling to find the Truth, but he needs help. How can other characters show him how it's done instead of just telling him about everything?

____

____

____

____

Question 3: As the Protagonist enters the new Adventure World of the Second Act, write down his true feelings about this transition.

____

____

____

____

____

____

Question 4: The protagonist is still clinging to an old Lie-based belief to reach his goal; what are those beliefs?

____

____

____

____

____

Question 5: Think and discuss why are these old Lie-based actions proving less useful in the Second Act than they were during your First.

____

____

____

____

____

____

THE MIDPOINT

The Protagonist has struggled with the cognitive dissonance caused by reality not matching up to their idealistic view. They have finally realized that what they thought was true might actually just be another opinion. Still, this new information isn't easy to accept because it runs cross-purposes with the seemingly perfect state of being, which makes the prospect of failure simply out of the question.

At the midpoint of their journey, the character is forced to confront their lie and desperately wants everything else, including themselves and their beliefs, to fit into this new understanding of reality. In Arthur Miller's *The Death of a Salesman*, Willy Loman's lie (or what he believes to be his truth) is the myth of success fashioned into his 'reality' by reconstructing memories. Being successful as a salesman and earning his son's respect are his wants. The edifice of his lies receives a severe jolt when his affair is discovered by Biff, and he loses all respect for him. Willy's inability to come to terms with the truth of his existence that no matter how hard he tries, he cannot live his American dream in reality halfway through the play prepares us for the inadvertent tragic end.

From this point onwards, all eyes are open wide, seeing how darkly complicated things really get.

Exercise: Answer the following questions about the Midpoint in your story.

Question 1: Describe the event of your story's Midpoint.

____

____

____

____

____

____

Question 2: How can we make this centerpiece scene as "big" and impressive-looking?

____

____

____

____

Question 3: Which of the many plans has your protagonist been executing to achieve his goal? The first half is full of Lie-based tactics, but by now, it should be clear that these are useless. It's time for some realizations and adjustments as we near our midpoint!

____

____

____

____

THE SECOND HALF OF THE SECOND ACT

The character finally understands the truth in the second half of their disillusionment arc. It is a truth that can drag them down into darkness but one which will allow for new beginnings and opportunities if confronted with courage, as happens in the case of a positive arc.

Exercise 1: Can you answer the questions about the Second Half of the Second Act?

Question 1: What does the character learn about the Truth at Midpoint? How is he reacting to it?

____

____

____

____

____

Question 2: The Moment of Truth provided your character with a new set of tools that have helped him make better progress toward what he wants.

____

____

____

____

____

Question 3: Is the lie still very much present in this character's life? Can you shed some light on this?

____

____

____

____

____

THE THIRD PLOT POINT

The Third Plot Point always has a deathly feel. The character is brought to face with their own mortality—either because their life is threatened or when all hope seems lost.

THE FIRST HALF OF THE THIRD ACT

The character's life is turned upside down when they finally understand the truth. All the lies are exposed as dysfunctional, and there's nothing left to cling onto but an empty hope that things will get better soon enough. The character's his final, and most crucial dilemma is to decide whether to surrender entirely to darkness or make a truce with a truth that may be difficult but could be the last straw.

Exercise: Answer the following questions in your story about the First Half of the Third Act

Question 1: Why not make things worse for your character after they've already hit rock bottom in the Third Plot Point and pick things from there onwards?

Question 2: Does the character have reason to regret his decision? Did he think of something else when acknowledging the truth?

Question 3: What will your character do after being healed? How can he gain control over his realization and grow with a new goal of approaching life?

____

____

____

____

____

Question 4: How can you ensure that your character is never quite satisfied with the Lie?

The best way to do this would be by constantly surprising him and giving him in-universe motivation for why they're so quick to trigger when it comes down to a choice between two possible outcomes.

____

____

____

____

____

THE CLIMAX

Do you remember the way your character was in the beginning? What he believed and how deeply he embraced it at first. Well, look back on what made him change—and think about where this all leads towards him!

The Lie your character embraced, in the beginning, should point you to an obvious culmination.

Question 1: What does your character do to show that he has changed before the Climax?

____

____

____

____

Question 2: Write down the final confrontation between the protagonist and their opponent will take place in what form?

____

____

____

____

____

____

Question 3: Where exactly does the Climax even take place?

____

____

____

Question 4: The final confrontation allows your protagonist to prove they have rejected lies, but how?

____

____

____

____

THE RESOLUTION

The closing scene of a story is often what drives home the character's final state. It could be anything from death, insanity, or prison. In Willy Loman's case, it's suicide; in Oedipus's case, it's self-blinding; in the case of King Lear, it's insanity. The end contrasts how the character had started out, riding the horse of their false idealisms, lies, or, as we call it, their 'truth.' The seriousness of their end is the manifestation of the extent of their inability to come to terms with reality.

CREATIVE EXERCISES

The ordinary world of your story can represent the lie your character believes, best if it is a place that symbolizes what we know to be true in our lives. For instance, imagine an adventure where you are transported into another reality with far less gravity or some other fundamental difference from how things work here on Earth—a utopia built upon illusions just as surely as any fairy tale.

Here is something you should think about :

1. Why is this character so committed to devaluing the Truth?

____

____

____

____

____

2. The Lie's Normal World is appealing, but why? What could be a fair reason for that?

3. What will happen to your character at the end of their story? Will they achieve victory or defeat, and why do you think so?

4. How are the supporting characters resonating with your
Protagonist? What is his response?

CHAPTER 4
THE NEGATIVE CHANGE ARC TYPE 2: FALL

The fall arc is one of the most tragic character arcs. Most of the iconic tragic heroes' characters follow the fall arc in which the protagonist is so infected with a lie that they can't extricate themselves from its clasp and may end up losing their mind or their lives.

THE LIE YOUR CHARACTER BELIEVES

In a Fall Arc, the protagonist will start believing in an incorrect and damaging view of themselves or their world. But, unlike other arcs where this is only temporary before they find something more substantial to believe in (as in the case of a positive change arc), they cling on to their original mistake more forcefully, to disastrous, self-debilitating outcomes. They see the flimsiness of their lies and recognize the alternative truth but are constitutionally incapable of making peace with or growing to embrace the truth. Instead, they prefer sinking with their ship!

Exercise 1: Can you write three possible variations of the Lie Your Character Believes? Be specific and clear while stating them.

Exercise 2: Choose one variation out of those 5 variations that will be the primary Lie for your character's arc. Write the one that best influences the storyline.

Exercise 3: Explain how the character's lie, a pretense, or an act is put on for the world that he lives in. His inner struggle with himself shows through his exterior actions and choices, which are often unpredictable to others because they do not know what motivates him behind closed doors; if someone were able to see through this person's facade, then there might be a greater understanding of their true feelings or thoughts, but everyone only sees whatever persona fits best at any given time - even friends who claim otherwise!

SYMPTOMS OF THE LIE

Your characters' actions and reactions to the different situations are symptomatic of their lies. They are often products of their fear or desire for something they want instead of what they need. Macbeth commits the crime—the murder of Duncan—which opens a can of worms. He goes on from crime to crime and guilt to guilt, which in his case, is not just a manifestation or symptom of the lie of ambition but also proof that he will sink with the ship and not jump off, even though he sees through the lie.

Question 1: Pick up the symptoms that are present in your character's lie.

- Fear

- Extreme hurt

- Ego

- Guilt

- Shame

- Secrets from the past

- Anger

- Shy

- Disappointed

YOUR CHARACTER'S GHOST

When a character's Ghost from the character's past continues to trouble him in the present, it can be difficult for that person to overcome what happened. A common type of "ghost" haunts someone because they cannot move on or successfully embrace truth while still believing in the lies.

For example, you might see this sort of thing sometimes referred to as "the wound." It's usually something shocking and traumatic and disturbing. In the case of Lady Macbeth, it is signified by her sleepwalking, insanity—seeing blood on her hands—culminating in her death.

Exercise 1: Can you state three events where your character feels motivated toward believing in his Lie? What has led to this?

____

____

____

____

Exercise 2: Sure that you know more about your Character's Ghost! Try answering these questions now:

Question 1: Which of your ideas for a backstory will be the most valuable primary motivating wound in terms of how you develop as an individual?

____

____

____

____

Question 2: How did the Ghost create or enable the Lie Your Character Believes by making you believe in things that aren't true?

Question 3: The character will try to use the Lie as a defense mechanism when they get caught up with the Ghost. In a way, how will the character support the Ghost and believe in it?

Question 4: How is the Lie and Ghost so thematically connected with each other in the story?

———————————————————————————————

———————————————————————————————

———————————————————————————————

———————————————————————————————

———————————————————————————————

Question 5: How would you rate the character's relationship with the Ghost? What do you think it is? Deep, strong, or weak?

———————————————————————————————

———————————————————————————————

———————————————————————————————

———————————————————————————————

———————————————————————————————

Question 6: The Ghost character is an intriguing presence in the story. He or she never speaks, but their silent intervention causes major events throughout "The Haunting." Why do you think it remains so relevant for the readers?

____

____

____

____

____

Question 7: What's the best way to present the Ghost in this story to your readers?

____

____

____

____

____

THE THING YOUR CHARACTER NEEDS

The protagonist in a fall arc desperately needs the truth from the very beginning. They suffer from their inability to extricate themselves from the trap of lies. In the case of Macbeth, a distortion of truth comes in the form of the riddles of the witches, which instead of exposing the lies—the futility of his ambition—ignites them.

These characters deserve truth more than any other characters following a different change arc. Another instance is Karna from the

Mahabharata. He deserved to know the truth about his identity from the very beginning, but instead, his quest for identity and a false assurance of social respectability and kinship provided by Duryodhan entraps him in the lie of lifetime loyalty. So, even after knowing his truth, his real identity—that he was the half-brother of the Pandavas—and that Duryodhan was fighting the battle for all the wrong causes, he did not change sides. He consciously embraced his imminent fall by siding with the lies. But could he have had a different change arc if he had always known the secret of his identity?

Exercise 1: Explain the three variations of the Truth that will make the character believe that Lie is not what will make him succeed ahead, and it is high time that he should realize this.

Exercise 2: Write down three possible ways your story's Truth is precisely what the character wants. It would be great if you could describe the event in clarity.

____

____

____

____

____

____

THE THING YOUR CHARACTER WANTS

What the protagonist wants is often a temporary relief, not a complete cure of their wounds, and hence, they never truly heal. This is because they're too engrossed in the events on the outside when in reality, they should be more focused on the inside.

The thing that drives our main character forward isn't always beneficial. It's primarily destructive because it's motivated by their lie. Upon closer inspection, issues such as moral compass failure could arise, which makes all their efforts futile.

Exercise 1: What are your character's deep, primal desires? What is it that they want more than anything else in this world or any other one for that matter? These aren't just goals- these will influence the specific story goal you select!

____

____

____

____

____

____

Exercise 2: There are desires that originate from primal desires, and how do you think each of these desires arises from Symptoms of Lie?

____

____

____

____

____

Exercise 3: What is the one thing your character wants more than anything else? What drives them to take up a cause and fight for it, even when others think they cannot succeed at achieving this goal? The answer lies in understanding what specific desire motivates him: love, money, or something else.

____

____

____

____

Exercise 4: Why not be a little more specific? What is your character's goal in this story? Your choices might include finding adventure, proving themselves to others, or just trying something new altogether! Make sure that you consider which one best guides the plot and theme of what will happen next.

____

____

____

____

Exercise 5: What is your character's primary goal in this story? What do they want more than anything else, and how will you achieve it if possible? Be sure to choose the option that best represents their desires while still being a worthwhile goal for them personally or professionally as well!

____

____

____

____

____

____

THE CHARACTERISTIC MOMENT

The characteristic moment is your protagonist's big debut. They step onto the stage and shine at that moment when readers know exactly why they're going to follow this character through all of his trials, both good and bad ones! The characteristic moment should give away the defining trait (in Macbeth's case, his military prowess and ambition) and set the stage for a journey towards actualizing the (false) goals by acting on their characteristic traits.

Exercise 1: To create the perfect Characteristic Moment, you need to know something about your character.

Question 1: Can you describe the character's role here in the story? If he is in the main lead as a Protagonist or Antagonist? Is he a mentor, supporting character, or someone else? Also, can you name it?

____

____

____

____

____

Question 2: Estimated age of your character?

____

____

____

Question 3: Nationality of your character (make it interesting)

____

____

____

Question 4: Your Character's occupation or some traits that can define his primary identity? (Businessman, smart, rebel, high on self-esteem)

____

____

____

____

____

Question 5: Define your character's physical characteristics (e.g., Birthmark, injury).

____

____

____

____

____

Question 6: Explain any 4 personality traits of your character that can best describe him and help readers connect with him. (Kind, gentlemen, witty, angry, likable).

____

____

____

____

____

Question 7: Describe one crucial personality trait of your character that best explains him. Talk about its virtues or skill or anything that you think is an essential yet impactful trait.

____

____

____

____

____

Question 8: How can you help readers connect with him through sympathy, relatability, or anything interesting? Try to find a connection here.

THE NORMAL WORLD

The normal world is what grounds the opening of your story in a concrete setting. It provides context for readers, but it isn't just about that. Macbeth's normal world is the world in and out of battlefields and royal courts. It's a world of martial prowess and political power. The norms and traditions within this society shape how characters behave and help create an unhappy yet complacent or apathetic tone throughout their unhappiness. Hence Macbeth's ambition and his 'end justifies the means' Machiavellean's attempt to pursue that ambition is pretty much a product of his 'normal world' (or at least what he perceives to be the normal world).

The normal world is the setting of your story, and it needs to be established clearly at its beginning so that all changes can have meaning.

Exercise: Answer the following questions about the Normal World in your story.

Question 1: Describe the physical or exterior settings of the Normal World.

Question 2: So the Normal World must have significance with the Lie that your character believes in. How will you describe that?

THE FIRST ACT

The fall arc is all about how the character deals with their Ghost throughout the story; so if it controls everything from what they want (or think they want, which is most of the time different from what they need) and what their next move will be, they are probably going down!

Exercise 1: Answer the following questions in the story First Act.

Question 1: Can you dramatize the character's Lie to create some serious thrill about it? A great hook for the readers?

____

____

____

____

____

Question 2: Show the character's contentment in the Lie and his real or idealistic view of the world.

____

____

____

____

____

Question 3: Write how you will show or present the Thing Your Character Wants and Needs.

____

____

____

____

____

Question 4: Can you write that part where the character in the Characteristic Moment gets a hint about the Lie?

____

____

____

____

____

Question 5: The Lie will be readily evident in his Normal World, but how would you show that in the story?

____

____

____

____

____

Question 6: What are some ways you can reinforce the Lie throughout the First Act? State any 4 ways.

____

____

____

____

____

Question 7: Can you hint about the character's inability with the truth and throw some light on the same?

____

____

____

____

THE FIRST PLOT POINT

The First Plot Point will frequently be positive—something seemingly excellent or exciting happens to the character. In Act, I scene iii of *Macbeth,* we meet Macbeth as a military hero, hailed by the three witches as the Thane of Glamis, of Cawdor, and then as the king. He is taken aback, but the witches disappear without further clarification. The following two other characters enter with the news that he has been awarded the title of Thane of Cawdor. Not just are things looking up for this character, but getting the title after the prophecy is a kind of reaffirmation of his ambitions—one part of the prophecy comes true; hence the other part, about becoming the king, seems to be plausible. This ignites the ambition and undoes the trapdoor to moral degeneracy, which he follows till the end.

Hence, after the seeming happiness, things start getting worse for the fall arc character—they descend into the darkness to create proper awareness within themselves about what needs fixing (aka "descending") before it's too late. But do they act on that awareness?

Question 1: So you know that the character has left the Normal World, what should be that event when this takes place? Explain that central conflict.

____

____

____

____

____

Question 2: How are you planning to make this event exciting for readers?

____

____

____

____

____

Question 3: What decision did your character make that led him up to the First Plot Point, taking at least partial responsibility for what happens?

____

____

____

____

____

THE FIRST HALF OF THE SECOND ACT

The first half of the second act is a response or reaction to the character's response to the first plot point. They suffer the consequences of continuing to believe in and use their lie but won't let go. The truth hits them hard that the lie is making their life difficult, but it is far more difficult for them to acknowledge, accept, and make peace with the truth.

THE MIDPOINT

At the midpoint, it's time for the character to take an irrevocable action based on lies to launch them into a space from where there's no coming back (or crawling up). In Macbeth's case, once he commits the murder of Duncan in his castle, there is no coming back—the fall becomes imminent from this point onwards.

THE SECOND HALF OF THE SECOND ACT

The tragic premise of the fall arc indicates a progression from bad to worse in the second half. Whatever your character's lie was at first, by now, they are neck-deep into it and become exactly what you did not want them to be!

THE THIRD PLOT POINT

The third plot point in a fall arc brings the character not to their most significant defeat yet—instead, there's a surface-level victory that comes at a price. In Macbeth's case, he becomes the king but loses his peace of mind, is haunted by guilt, and has to witness his wife's degeneration into insanity and, finally, her death.

THE FIRST HALF OF THE THIRD ACT

A fall arc character is, most of the time, a tragic hero who is wronged in some way and hence often more sinned against than sinning. Take Karna's example—his actions, no matter how questionable as per the reader's moral compass, never take him out of the scope of the reader's sympathy. So this part of the plot ensures that no matter how 'dark' their actions may seem, these characters will find some kind of justice or closure with their ultimate defeat!

THE CLIMAX

The climactic moment in a fall arc will progress with an overwhelming sense of inevitable destruction. The character has already fully and irretrievably sold themself to the worst possible version of their lie, knowing that they cannot turn back from this fate but pushing forward nonetheless determined for what could be the last effort before death or damnation. In *Macbeth,* the third act of the third scene marks the climax—Fleance escapes, and Macbeth has not truly gained what he was striving for. His fears and hallucinations make him lose all control; he is on a killing spree culminating in his own doom.

THE RESOLUTION

The Fall Arc often ends with little leftover business for readers, leaving them wanting more instead of feeling satisfied or fulfilled. The resolution comes with the tragic end of a character with whom the reader could relate, despite their flaws. Hence a dreadful but imminent catastrophe though does not come as a shock but leaves the reader/audience shaken.

CREATIVE EXERCISES

The Fall Arc is about the character progressing from one Lie to a worse Lie. Brainstorm a list of increasingly "worse" Lies the character might embrace if he starts down that path.

Here is something you should think about :

1. Why is the main character not yet out of this world? Why has he or she not tried to escape their Normal World life and move on to another phase?

____

____

____

____

____

2. Will your character be able to withstand the Lie's tests?

____

____

____

____

____

3. Will his actions have an irreversible effect on others? Are there any chances of damage?

____

____

____

____

4. How will your protagonist get what he/she wants? He might come up to fight with evil forces to achieve his goal.

____

____

CHAPTER 5

THE NEGATIVE CHANGE ARC TYPE 3: CORRUPTION

The corruption arc is the degeneration of a character from moral strength (or neutrality) to moral weakness; the character, despite being in complete knowledge of the truth, chooses the lie. It's hard not to feel sorry as they throw away their chance at redemption because it would be easier just staying on this side of darkness.

THE TRUTH YOUR CHARACTER BELIEVES

In a corruption arc, the character begins with a staunch rejection of what they end up doing later. The idea is to show that the character starts with a different approach to life than he later adopts. A classic example can be the character of Harvey Dent in Christopher Nolan's *The Dark Knight*.

Exercise 1: Can you write down three possible variations where the character believes in the Truth? The variations should be specific and clear.

____

____

____

____

____

Exercise 2: Choose one variation out of those three variations that will be the primary Lie for your character's arc. Write the one that best influences the storyline.

____

____

____

____

YOUR CHARACTER'S GHOST

The Ghost in your character's past prevents them from embracing the truth, putting everything else behind.

Sometimes it's an event, a trauma, or a memory that can haunt someone forever because they don't know how to deal with their pain. The more devastating thing was when this occurred - whether it was a traumatic experience that scarred them emotionally for life (the big Lie) or just one wrong decision snowballing into moral degeneration and the final catastrophe.

THE THING YOUR CHARACTER NEEDS

The character in a corruption arc usually starts with an all-consuming desire which is gradually groomed into an obsession that leads him further away from the truth until there's no return. Everything was done for seemingly reasonable purposes but became wrong decisions with significant consequences.

THE NORMAL WORLD

The character's Normal World will be a place of peace and hope. When the audience is first introduced to Harvey Dent in *The Dark Knight*, he symbolizes perfection—a crusader against organized crime, the morally upright district attorney, and a suitor for Rachel. The opening scene should show how great life was before anything changed, and Nolan does that with the mass trial scene, the introductory scene where Harvey is launched as the incorruptible White Knight of Gotham. This makes the eventual moral degeneration more of a shock.

Question 1: Can you describe the world around which you will set up the character's arc?

____

____

____

____

____

Question 2: Describe the truth about your character's exterior world and how it can be a metaphor for the things they reject.

____

____

____

____

____

Question 3: What are some ways in which we can see or experience the protagonist's 'before' state?

____

____

____

____

____

Question 4: What setting is best for your character's Ghost? To find out, you need to know their history. What events, in particular, do they remember from before becoming a ghost, and how does this affect them now that they're one?

____

____

____

____

____

Question 5: Why has the Protagonist never chosen to leave before the Normal World?

____

____

____

____

____

Question 6: The Normal World is a place of normality, where people go about their everyday lives without much adventure or excitement. The Adventure world, on the other hand, has its own share of dangers that can be found anywhere, from dangerous animals to treacherous terrain; it's what you make happen!

____

____

____

THE CHARACTERISTIC MOMENT

The characteristic moment in a corruption arc should hint at what's to come. It is a subtle hint to the character's true self and their potential for corruption. The tone here hints more towards "something dark," which will lead them down an inevitable path toward destruction.

· · ·

Exercise 1: What is your character's name? What does this person like to do in their free time, and how did it come about (i.e., did they grow up playing sports)? Who are some of the people important enough for them not just to work but also to form part of social life outside the workplace--friends at home who often visit each other over dinner etc.? Do you know anything else relevant such as birthplace/parents' careers before moving on.

____

____

____

____

____

____

Question 1: Can you describe the character's role here in the story? If he is in the main lead as a Protagonist or Antagonist? Is he a mentor, supporting character, or someone else? Also, can you name it?

Question 2: Estimated age of your character?

Question 3: Nationality of your character (interesting, right?)

____

____

____

Question 4: Your Character's occupation or some traits that can define his primary identity? (Businessman, innovative, rebel, high on self-esteem)

____

____

____

____

Question 5: Define your character's physical characteristics (e.g., Birthmark, injury).

____

____

____

____

Question 6: Explain any 4 personality traits of your character that can best describe him and help readers connect with him. (Kind, gentlemen, witty, angry, likable).

____

____

____

____

Question 7: Describe one crucial personality trait of your character that best explains him. Talk about its virtues or skill or anything that you think is an essential yet impactful trait.

____

____

____

____

____

Question 8: How can you help readers connect with him through sympathy, relatability, or anything interesting? Try to find a connection here.

____

____

____

____

____

. . .

Question 9: Can you describe the character's story goal and 'Thing.'

____

____

____

____

____

____

THE FIRST ACT

The plot featuring a character in the corruption arc must develop both truths and lie, so much so that each is always accompanied by the other's reflection. This helps readers understand how these two forces have shaped the character's world while also establishing what might be at stake if they pursue the path of the lie.

Every decision the character makes comes at the price of losing something precious. Every choice has its own setbacks and rewards attached to it. The first major decision and action that will force them out of the normal world won't happen until the end of act one. But, up until then, an increase in personal discomfort is key to leading our

Protagonist on a path away from what's valid with all truthful opportunities at hand!

THE FIRST PLOT POINT

Something happens, some trigger that sets the character on the road to moral decay. They are still pretty idealistic, but the sudden jolt to their normal world forces them to make questionable moral decisions as they try to find a solution to the crisis.

THE FIRST HALF OF THE SECOND ACT

The second act in a negative change arc is similar to positive ones. The character is ratted out of their comfort zone into a moral dilemma where they must confront lies themselves and learn more about their latent power over them. The power of the lie gets stronger. In the *Mahabharata,* Karna's world changes when Duryodhana offers him the Kingdom of Angha; the lies about his parentage force him to embrace another lie, the lie of social acceptability with the promise of a royal title. But respect doesn't come to Karna so quickly. However, the false hope of respect makes him swear his allegiance to his 'friend' Duryodhana, whom he supports at the cost of a compromised sense of morality. As we go deeper into the plot, a corruption arc character begins to embrace lies more vehemently to the point of complete rejection of truth.

THE MIDPOINT

As the moral decay escalates, the character also encounters a moment of truth at the midpoint, which is an opportunity for them to save their souls. Karna can see through the futility of Duryodhana's claims to the Hastinapur throne, he knows his actions are premised on ego, stubborn claims to superiority, and a staunch antipathy towards his cousins, the Pandavas, still Karna will not waver from being an accomplice to Duryodhana. Even after knowing his true identity, he declines the offer to fight the battle from the Pandavas' side. The truth of his birth was another lie to lure him away to the Pandavas' side, but this was not the only reason why he rejected it. He rejects it out of another lie—the lie of friendship and loyalty towards Duryodhana, fed by the trauma of childhood abandonment and rejection from his mother Kunti.

Unlike the characters in the positive change arc who take the shot at truth and redeem themselves, the corruption arc character at this point totally abandons truth, despite having complete knowledge of it.

THE SECOND HALF OF THE SECOND ACT

Now that the total rejection of truth is complete, the character will start pursuing their goal with a renewed urgency. Truth no longer stands between him and what he wants, which is nothing but destruction for those who get in his way!

THE THIRD PLOT POINT

In the third plot point, the character faces the most significant defeat yet—but victory awaits them despite that. The thing he wants most is now within reach, however, at a price too high to pay for such superficial gain. In Nolan's The Dark Knight, Harvey Dent's reality surfaces in the event of Rachel's death. He embraces chaos and becomes two-faced Harvey, a symbol of moral decadence, and continues the killing spree until he dies. He rejects all the chances to redeem his image of the 'White Knight' of Gotham—what's worse, the corruption arc character refuses to acknowledge the moral decadence.

THE FIRST HALF OF THE THIRD ACT

The character has rejected the truth and any chance of redemption. Without any truth to guide them, nothing is stopping them from total degeneracy. They may turn on those close before when all they were trying was to help, but their suggestions will go unheeded because no one can reach deep enough into our cores when we have already made our choices consciously.

THE CLIMAX

The climax is where everything finally and fully falls apart. The character's last desperate push to use the lie will achieve either an outer victory or inner wholeness with no true sense of fulfillment until they realize what really matters—the truth.

However, this momentary realization can be a redeeming feature that should be skipped if you want to create the corruption arc. Instead, the character should take full ownership of their choices and remain 'justified' in their own head.

THE RESOLUTION

The death of the corruption arc character can have a significant impact on the people around them. For example, the people of Gotham believed in Harvey Dent as a symbol of order. So his degeneration into chaos would shake them to the core. They might go through disillusionment arcs or start believing in something new, which can be something even darker. Perhaps to avoid this ripple effect, Batman embraces the image of the dark knight and lets Harvey's clean image linger on as a collective memory of faith in order and goodness.

CREATIVE EXERCISES

Think about this, what if your character was not strong enough in his initial Truth to resist the call of Lie?

Why did he give up so quickly and let himself be seduced by a false promise, even though it meant leaving everything behind him? Why could this person not see through all that propaganda without being too stubborn or loyal-minded like some people tend (oftentimes) towards becoming victims themselves when they believe every word coming out of those mouths before ever thinking critically about what's said or doesn't say?!

Here is what you should focus at:

1. Imagine that the Truth is nourishing food, but it doesn't make the character feel at home in their Normal World. Why is that happening to him?

____

____

____

____

____

2. So, let's say your character is biased towards the Lie, but why?

---

3. What Moment of Truth allows your character to embrace the truth? Why and how does he reject it at this Midpoint in his journey through life's pages?

---

4. What's worse than being powerless? rising up from the Third Plot Point wiser and more robust, but still unable to do anything about your inner or outer conflict.

CONCLUSION

No matter how good a story is, If the characters don't breathe life into it, then it's just ink on paper. Your characters are there to create and push it forward with their actions, dialogue, and thoughts—in short, by being them! Readers can experience the world you create in and out through your characters. The positive / negative change arcs or the flat arc give your characters a vast emotional range which helps the readers connect at a human level with your story.

If you have made it up to the end of this book, you know which blueprint suits the characters who feature in your story and plan accordingly.

The workspace in this book is to help you ponder and practice as much as possible before launching your own characters in the world of your book. Let's create character arcs together!

MORE FROM
JOHN S WARNER

Writing Strategies

The Secrets to Creating Character Arcs

The Secrets to Outlining Your Novel

Just One a Day Writing Prompts

The Secrets to Creating Character Arcs Workbook

Available on Amazon.com

BIBLIOGRAPHY

5 Important Characters to Have in Every Story. (n.d.). NY Book Editors. Retrieved December 1, 2021, from https://nybookeditors.com/2018/01/5-important-characters-tohave-in-every-story/

Allen, K. M. (2018, March 2). *Character Dos and Don'ts*. K.M. Allan. Retrieved December 1, 2021, from https://kmallan.com/2018/03/02/character-dos-and-donts/

Author Learning Centre. (n.d.). *How to Structure a Story: The Fundamentals of Narrative - article*. Retrieved January 5, 2022, from https://www.authorlearningcenter.com/writing/fiction/w/plot-planning/6366/how-to-structure-a-storythe-fundamentals-of-narrative---article

Autocrit Staff. (n.d.). *Making Minor Characters Matter*. AutoCrit. Retrieved December 1, 2021, from https://www.autocrit.com/blog/making-minor-characters-matter/

Beemgee Staff. (n.d.). *Plot vs Character*. Beemgee. Retrieved December 1, 2021, from https://www.beemgee.com/blog/plot-vs-character/

Bianchi, N. (2021, July 24). *5 Writing Exercises for Creating Compelling Characters*. Nicole Bianchi. Retrieved December 1, 2021, from https://nicolebianchi.com/writing-exercisescharacter-development/

Brody, J. (2018). *Save the Cat! Writes a Novel: The Last Book On Novel Writing You'll Ever Need*. Ten Speed Press.

Brown, K. (2015, March 1). *The Key to a Great Story – Combining Characters and Plot*. A Young Writers Notebook.

Retrieved December 1, 2021, from https://

katherinebrownwriting.wordpress.com

Bunting, J. (n.d.). *Ten Secrets To Write Better Stories*. The Write Practice.Com. Retrieved December 1, 2021, from https://thewritepractice.com/write-story/

Chase, J. (n.d.). *Plot and Structure: How to Use Structure and Subplot to Add Suspense*. The Write Practice. Retrieved December 1, 2021, from https://thewritepractice.com/plot-structure/

Cook, E., Barker, D., & Hunt, C. (2020). *Build Better Characters: The psychology of backstory & how to use it in your writing to hook readers (Creative Academy Guides for Writers)*. Creative Academy fr Writers.

Cook, R. (2008, June 21). *Plot vs Structure*. Rick Cooks Notebook. Retrieved January 5, 2022, from http://rickcooks.blogspot.com/2008/07/plot-vs-structure.html

DuMairier, J. A. (2017). *What makes a good story*. Thanet Writers. Retrieved December 1, 2021, from https://thanetwriters.com/essay/troubleshooting/what-makes-a-good-story/

Ennen, D. (n.d.). *What makes a good fiction Book*. Street Directory. Retrieved December 1, 2021, from https://www.

streetdirectory.com/travel_guide/154225/writing/what_makes_a_good_fiction_-book.html

Flowers, A. J. (2015, September 8). *The Dos and Don'ts of Character Development.* AJFlowers.Com. Retrieved December 1, 2021, from https://aj-flowers.com/2015/09/08/the-dosand-donts-of-character-development/

Graf, R. (2019, October 12). *The 6 Basic Key Elements of Fiction Writing.* Hobby Lark. Retrieved December 1, 2021, from https://hobbylark.com/writing/Basic-Key-Elements-ofFiction-Writing

Humpage, A. J. (2016, March 12). *The Importance of Supporting Characters.* All Write Fiction Advice. Retrieved December 1, 2021, from http://allwritefictionad-vice.blogspot.com/2016/ 03/the-importance-of-supporting-characters.html

Irvine, I. (n.d.). *55 Ways to Create Compelling Characters.* Ian Irvine. Retrieved December 1, 2021, from https://www.ianirvine.com/for-writers/article-3-create-great-characters/

iuniverse staff. (n.d.). *20 Writing Tips from Fiction Authors.* Iuniverse. Retrieved December 1, 2021, from https://www.

iuniverse.com/en/resources/writing-and-editing/20writing-tips-from-fiction-authors

Jackal Editing. (n.d.). *The 4 Main Plot Points: What They Are and How to Use Them.* Retrieved January 5, 2022, from http:// www.jackalediting.com/the-4-main-plot-points/

Jarvis, J. (2014). *Crafting the Character Arc.* Beating Windward Press.

Jordan. (n.d.-a). *Novel characters: 15 top character creation tips.* NowNovel. Retrieved December 1, 2021, from https://www. nownovel.com/blog/novel-characters-15-tips/

Jordan. (n.d.-b). *What makes a good story? 10 elements.* Now Novel. Retrieved January 5, 2022, from https://www. nownovel.com/blog/what-makes-a-good-story/

Kidder, H. L. (2021, October 1). *How to Write a Character Arc (With a Writing Exercise).* Self Publishing School. Retrieved December 1, 2021, from https://self-publishingschool.-com/ character-arc/

Kieffer, K. (2020, April 11). *How to Craft Positive Character Arcs For Your Novel.* Well-Storied. Retrieved December 1, 2021, from https://www.well-storied.-com/blog/craftstrong-character-arcs

King, T. (2011, March 1). *11 Functions of Plot.* Be the Story. Retrieved December 1, 2021, from http://bethestory.com/ 2011/03/01/11-functions-of-plot

Maguire, A. (2017, December 27). *Structural Elements: The Basic Tools of the Writer Part 1.* The Writing Cooperative. Retrieved January 5, 2022, from https://writingcoop-erative.

com/structural-elements-the-basic-tools-of-the-writerpart-1-889a1599e369

MasterClass Staff. (2021a, September 8). *How to Develop a Fictional Character: 6 Tips for Writing Great Character.* MasterClass. Retrieved December 1, 2021, from https://www.

masterclass.com/articles/writing-tips-for-characterdevelopment

MasterClass Staff. (2021b, November 16). *6 Elements of Good Fiction Writing.* MasterClass. Retrieved December 1, 2021, from https://www.masterclass.com/articles/elements-ofgood-fiction-writing

Perry, A. K. (2017, September 11). *Three Major Roles of Minor Characters.* DiyMFA. Retrieved December 1, 2021, from https://diymfa.com/writing/three-major-roles-minorcharacters

Reedsy Blog. (2018, June 26). *What is a plot point?* Retrieved January 5, 2022, from https://blog.reedsy.com/plot-point/

Salao, C. (n.d.). *3 Types of Supporting Characters and How to Write Them Better*. T C K Publishing. Retrieved December 1, 2021, from https://www.tckpublishing.-com/types-ofsupporting-characters/

Scribendi. (n.d.). *The Golden Rules for a good plot*. Retrieved January 5, 2022, from https://www.scribendi.com/academy/ articles/goldenrulesforagoodplot.en.html

Sims, E. (2012, June 19). *7 Simple Ways to Make a Good Story Great*. Writers Digest. Retrieved December 1, 2021, from https://www.writersdigest.com/whats-new/7-simple-waysto-make-a-good-story-great

Smith, J. (2021, June 15). *How to find your novel's structure*. The Writer. Retrieved December 1, 2021, from https://www. writermag.com/improve-your-writing/revision-grammar/ find-novels-structure/

Stein, C. (2018, April 8). *Main Character vs. Supporting Characters in Story Development*. Think Written. Retrieved December 1, 2021, from https://thinkwritten.com/main-character-vs-supporting-characters/

Weiland, K. M. (2016). *Creating Character Arcs: The Masterful Author's Guide to Uniting Story Structure (Helping Writers Become Authors)* (Annotated ed.). PenForASword.

Weiland, K. M. (2017). *Creating Character Arcs Workbook: The Writer's Reference to Exceptional Character Development and Creative Writing (Helping Writers Become Authors Book 8)*. PenForASword Publishing.

Welcker, R. (n.d.). *Four Basic Principles in Writing Fiction*. Writing Commons. Retrieved December 1, 2021, from https://writingcommons.org/article/four-basic-principlesin-writing-fiction/

Yates-Martin, T. (2020, February 24). *10 Ways to Make the Reader Care about Your Protagonist*. Writers in the Storm.

Retrieved December 1, 2021, from https://

writersinthestormblog.com/2020/02/10-ways-to-makethe-reader-care-about-your-protagonist/

5 Important Characters to Have in Every Story. (n.d.). NY Book Editors. Retrieved December 1, 2021, from https:// nybookeditors.com/2018/01/5-important-characters-tohave-in-every-story/

Allen, K. M. (2018, March 2). *Character Dos and Don'ts*. K.M. Allan. Retrieved December 1, 2021, from https://kmallan. com/2018/03/02/character-dos-and-donts/

Author Learning Centre. (n.d.). *How to Structure a Story: The Fundamentals of Narrative - article*. Retrieved January 5, 2022, from https://www.authorlearningcenter.com/writing/ fiction/w/plot-planning/6366/how-to-structure-a-storythe-fundamentals-of-narrative---article

Autocrit Staff. (n.d.). *Making Minor Characters Matter*. AutoCrit. Retrieved December 1, 2021, from https://www. autocrit.com/blog/making-minor-characters-matter/

Beemgee Staff. (n.d.). *Plot vs Character*. Beemgee. Retrieved December 1, 2021, from https://www.beemgee.com/blog/ plot-vs-character/

Bianchi, N. (2021, July 24). *5 Writing Exercises for Creating Compelling Characters*. Nicole Bianchi. Retrieved December 1, 2021, from https://nicolebianchi.com/writing-exercisescharacter-development/

Brody, J. (2018). *Save the Cat! Writes a Novel: The Last Book On Novel Writing You'll Ever Need*. Ten Speed Press.

Brown, K. (2015, March 1). *The Key to a Great Story – Combining Characters and Plot*. A Young Writers Notebook.

Retrieved December 1, 2021, from https:/ /

katherinebrownwriting.wordpress.com

Bunting, J. (n.d.). *Ten Secrets To Write Better Stories*. The Write Practice.Com. Retrieved December 1, 2021, from https:/ / thewritepractice.com / write-story /

Chase, J. (n.d.). *Plot and Structure: How to Use Structure and Subplot to Add Suspense*. The Write Practice. Retrieved December 1, 2021, from https://thewritepractice.com/plot structure/

Cook, E., Barker, D., & Hunt, C. (2020). *Build Better Characters: The psychology of backstory & how to use it in your writing to hook readers (Creative Academy Guides for Writers)*. Creative Academy fr Writers.

Cook, R. (2008, June 21). *Plot vs Structure*. Rick Cooks Notebook. Retrieved January 5, 2022, from http://rickcooks. blogspot.com/2008/07/plot-vs-structure.html

DuMairier, J. A. (2017). *What makes a good story*. Thanet Writers. Retrieved December 1, 2021, from https://thanetwriters. com/essay/troubleshooting/what-makes-a-good-story/

Ennen, D. (n.d.). *What makes a good fiction Book*. Street Directory. Retrieved December 1, 2021, from https://www.

streetdirectory.com/travel_guide/154225/ writing/what_makes_a_good_fiction_-book.html

Flowers, A. J. (2015, September 8). *The Dos and Don'ts of Character Development*. AJFlowers.Com. Retrieved December 1, 2021, from https:/ /aj-flowers.com/2015/09/08/the-dosand-donts-of-character-development/

Graf, R. (2019, October 12). *The 6 Basic Key Elements of Fiction Writing*. Hobby Lark. Retrieved December 1, 2021, from https://hobbylark.com/writing/Basic-Key-Elements-ofFiction-Writing

Humpage, A. J. (2016, March 12). *The Importance of Supporting Characters*. All Write Fiction Advice. Retrieved December 1, 2021, from http://allwritefictionadvice. blogspot.com/2016/ 03/the-importance-of-supporting-characters.html

Irvine, I. (n.d.). *55 Ways to Create Compelling Characters*. Ian Irvine. Retrieved December 1, 2021, from https://www.ianirvine.com/for-writers/article-3-create-great-characters/ iuniverse staff. (n.d.). *20 Writing Tips from Fiction Authors*. Iuniverse. Retrieved December 1, 2021, from https://www.

iuniverse.com/en/resources/writing-and-editing/20writing-tips-from-fiction-authors

Jackal Editing. (n.d.). *The 4 Main Plot Points: What They Are and How to Use Them*. Retrieved January 5, 2022, from http:/ / www.jackalediting.com/the-4-main-plot-points/

Jarvis, J. (2014). *Crafting the Character Arc*. Beating Windward Press.

Jordan. (n.d.-a). *Novel characters: 15 top character creation tips*. NowNovel. Retrieved December 1, 2021, from https:/ /www. nownovel.com/blog/novel-characters-15-tips/

Jordan. (n.d.-b). *What makes a good story? 10 elements*. Now Novel. Retrieved January 5, 2022, from https://www. nownovel.com/blog/what-makes-a-good-story/

Kidder, H. L. (2021, October 1). *How to Write a Character Arc (With a Writing Exercise)*. Self Publishing School. Retrieved December 1, 2021, from https://self-publishingschool. com/ character-arc/

Kieffer, K. (2020, April 11). *How to Craft Positive Character Arcs For Your Novel*. Well-Storied. Retrieved December 1, 2021, from https://www.well-storied.com/blog/craft strong-character-arcs

King, T. (2011, March 1). *11 Functions of Plot*. Be the Story. Retrieved December 1, 2021, from http://bethestory.com/ 2011/03/01/11-functions-of-plot

Maguire, A. (2017, December 27). *Structural Elements: The Basic Tools of the Writer Part 1*. The Writing Cooperative. Retrieved January 5, 2022, from https://writingcoopera tive.

com/structural-elements-the-basic-tools-of-the-writerpart-1-889a1599e369

MasterClass Staff. (2021a, September 8). *How to Develop a Fictional Character: 6 Tips for Writing Great Character*. MasterClass. Retrieved December 1, 2021, from https://www.

masterclass.com/articles/writing-tips-for-characterdevelopment

MasterClass Staff. (2021b, November 16). *6 Elements of Good Fiction Writing*. MasterClass. Retrieved December 1, 2021, from https://www.masterclass.com/articles/elements-ofgood-fiction-writing

Perry, A. K. (2017, September 11). *Three Major Roles of Minor Characters*. DiyMFA. Retrieved December 1, 2021, from https://diymfa.com/writing/three-major-roles-minorcharacters

Reedsy Blog. (2018, June 26). *What is a plot point?* Retrieved January 5, 2022, from https://blog.reedsy.com/plot-point/

Salao, C. (n.d.). *3 Types of Supporting Characters and How to Write Them Better*. T C K Publishing. Retrieved December 1, 2021, from https://www.tckpublishing.com/ types-ofsupporting-characters/

Scribendi. (n.d.). *The Golden Rules for a good plot*. Retrieved January 5, 2022, from https:// www.scribendi.com/academy/ articles/goldenrulesforagoodplot.en.html

Sims, E. (2012, June 19). *7 Simple Ways to Make a Good Story Great*. Writers Digest. Retrieved December 1, 2021, from https://www.writersdigest.com/whats-new/7-simple-waysto-make-a-good-story-great

Smith, J. (2021, June 15). *How to find your novel's structure*. The Writer. Retrieved December 1, 2021, from https://www. writermag.com/improve-your-writing/revi-sion-grammar/ find-novels-structure/

Stein, C. (2018, April 8). *Main Character vs. Supporting Characters in Story Development*. Think Written. Retrieved December 1, 2021, from https://thinkwritten.com/main character-vs-supporting-characters/

Weiland, K. M. (2016). *Creating Character Arcs: The Masterful Author's Guide to Uniting Story Structure (Helping Writers Become Authors)* (Annotated ed.). PenForASword.

Weiland, K. M. (2017). *Creating Character Arcs Workbook: The Writer's Reference to Excep-tional Character Development and Creative Writing (Helping Writers Become Authors Book 8)*. PenForASword Publishing.

Welcker, R. (n.d.). *Four Basic Principles in Writing Fiction*. Writing Commons. Retrieved December 1, 2021, from https://writingcommons.org/article/four-basic-princi plesin-writing-fiction/

Yates-Martin, T. (2020, February 24). *10 Ways to Make the Reader Care about Your Protagonist.* Writers in the Storm.
Retrieved December 1, 2021, from https://
writersinthestormblog.com/2020/02/10-ways-to-makethe-reader-care-about-your-protagonist/